# RETURN TO THE SUNLIGHT
A Story of Hope, Resilience, and Redemption

John Wayne Houston

Title page art by Naris Artyuenyong

Return to the Sunlight:
A Story of Hope, Resilience, and Redemption

©2025 John Wayne Houston
Published by Get Heard Publishing House,
an Elevated Missions PREP, Inc. company.
All rights reserved.

This book is protected under the copyright laws of the United States of America. Any reproduction or unauthorized use of the material herein is prohibited without the expressed written permission of the author.

Paperback: 978-1-964111-26-1
Hardcover: 978-1-964111-27-8

# Dedication

To God, your belief that I was still worthy of living, your grace, your mercy, and your carving out the right circumstances for my recovery and placing the right people in my life brought me through,

To my parents, George Houston and Rachel Houston, though you have gone from this world, your lessons on how to face challenges helped me make it through.

To my children, Marisa and Renee, your forgiveness allowed me to the be father I wanted to be.

To my grandchildren, your presence motivated me, and I love being your silly grandfather.

To Linda and Helen, your unconditional love fueled this turnaround.

To my boys, Marques and Isaiah, I have not forgotten you and continue to look for you till this day. You will always have a place in my heart.

To all my family and friends, who helped me stay on track, thank you.

To everyone who is still in their struggle, you can make it.

To the love ones of those who are still in their struggle, they can make it.

# Foreword

I first met John Houston on August 6, 2004, when he appeared before me in a Kitsap County Superior Court courtroom in Port Orchard, Washington. He was charged in criminal court with one count of Delivery of Controlled Substance and two counts of Possession of Cocaine. He was facing twenty months in prison. John had been an addict for thirty-six years, lost his marriage and home, and succumbed to a life of violence and homelessness on the streets of Bremerton, Washington. City and state parks had become his home when he wasn't couch surfing. He was an angry, hostile, and, unbeknownst to him, a broken man.

A few years earlier, I had formed our local Drug Court program, essentially a diversion model, trading chemical dependency treatment for incarceration. John wasn't the best candidate for our Drug Court program. Nevertheless, the Drug Court Team screened him and found that he met the technical criteria for admission (only recently had we expanded eligibility to allow delivery of controlled substances charges to petition for admission to our program). Despite many reasons to say "no" to his petition, I took a chance and admitted him to our Drug Court.

What were the odds he would be successful? It was not always smooth sailing. As he now reminds people, he didn't like me at first. After all, I held people accountable, and frankly, he made it difficult for me to like him.

Participants in our Drug Court attend court sessions each week for the first eighteen weeks, and it was there that I began to see the man behind the addiction. I saw a determination that had eluded John for thirty-six years – a man who longed for improvement and wanted to live up to his potential, becoming an asset to his family. Drug Court is a challenging program, requiring three random urine analyses per week, group and individual counseling sessions, community service, financial costs, and employment or education requirements. Most participants are unable to complete the program without being sanctioned for some violation within the year and a half. However, John was determined and completed the task without any sanctions. John had a chemical dependency counselor, Steve Khort, a long-haired Harley biker, who challenged John. John admitted that Steve was precisely the type of person, on the outside, that he would have fought for no reason.

As much as I would like to claim Drug Court accounted for his success, it was the birth of his granddaughter, Olivia Marie, on July 24, 2004, that provided John with the determination to be there for her, where he hadn't been available for his daughters and the rest of his family. That determination was fostered by John's daughter, Marisa, telling him that he'd never meet his granddaughter if he didn't change. John graduated from our Drug Court on January 27, 2006, but his journey didn't stop there. His goal was to be a chemical dependency counselor, to help troubled youth avoid repeating his life's pitfalls. I attended John's graduation from Olympic Junior College on June 16, 2008, at which time John introduced me to his granddaughter, Olivia. John went on to complete his training to become a chemical dependency counselor and eventually returned to his hometown of Renton, Washington. There, in his continuing effort to "give back" to the communities that support him, he founded the Renton Youth Advocacy Center, where he serves as the Director.

John sought more profound understanding of why and how his life had taken such a drastic detour for so many years. He had an abiding belief there was something underlying his life's choices. How had he been a star athlete in high school, destined for college athletic scholarships, and turned to drugs? Why had his family had such struggles? What had happened to his wonderful childhood, where he enjoyed his family's property and the life it provided? He now understands and seeks to address the trauma inflicted on his family so many years ago. He doesn't blame his addiction on it, but now sees how racism and pressured forced sale of the Houston family home and ten acres had destroyed his family and the loss of generational wealth.

I am proud to have stood along with John and his family in addressing this travesty in numerous public meetings. John and his family merely seek reparations for the wrong done to them. The Houston family is but one of many African American families that have lost property through the threat of condemnation, actual condemnation, and eminent domain. Because John pursued justice in the form of reparations or even a simple acknowledgement of the Houston's family tragedy, Washington State passed Senate Bill 5142, the Houston Eminent Domain Fairness Act. It won't do anything for the Houstons, but it will allow other families to repurchase condemned land if that land is not used for the intended purpose.

John was legally blind when he entered our Drug Court. His vision continues to deteriorate. It would be fitting for him to "see" justice for his family before it is too late. This book documents his and his family's journey. Hopefully, he will be able to see that return to sunlight.

*Jay Roof, Former Judge*
*Kitsap County Superior Court,*
*Port Orchard, WA*

# Table of Contents

Dedication

Foreword

## SECTION I
## DRIFTING FROM THE SUNLIGHT

**Chapter 1**
The Great Escape.................................................. 7

**Chapter 2**
An Idyllic Life Shattered............................... 11

**Chapter 3**
Friendships and Frustrations...................... 19

**Chapter 4**
The Breaking................................................... 29

## SECTION II
## BLOCKING THE SUNLIGHT

**Chapter 5**
Caught Up in the Cycle................................. 39

**Chapter 6**
I Lost It All......................................................45

**Chapter 7**
Losing Marques................................................55

**Chapter 8**
Losing Isaiah................................................... 61

**Chapter 9**
Losing Mom.................................................... 69

**Chapter 10**
Round Seven: You Lose................................... 75

## SECTION III
## FIGHTING FOR THE SUNLIGHT

**Chapter 11**
The Choice......................................................85

**Chapter 12**
The Steps........................................................ 93

**Chapter 13**
All In.............................................................. 101

**Chapter 14**
Success Unlocked...........................................105

**Chapter 15**
College Life....................................................115

**SECTION IV
LIVING IN THE SUNLIGHT**

**Chapter 16**
Carving the Path..................................................129

**Chapter 17**
One More Wrong to Right........................... 139

**Chapter 18**
My Challenge to the Future Ahead............147

**Special Acknowledgements**
..................................................................................151

# SECTION I
# DRIFTING FROM THE SUNLIGHT

# Chapter 1
# The Great Escape

No one knows how long my father remained hidden under that house. Some say it was a week. I am unsure of all the facts because I had not been born yet; however, I do know it was what prompted my parents to make the great escape. According to the stories I heard, an angry mob of white men was hunting for my father, whom they said had offended a white woman. At that time, my parents lived in Louisiana, part of the heart of the Deep South. Everyone knew then that this was a time when they held trials in the woods and issued immediate punishment through hanging. My father, who was married with four children at the time, needed to survive despite the injustice of their actions, so he hid until it was safe for him to resurface. When he finally emerged, he had decided that our family would no longer live in Louisiana. He wanted something better for himself, his wife, and the children they had together. Thus, he hopped a train and headed west to establish a new life for his family.

Not unlike those first pioneers who pushed west in search of a golden opportunity, my father headed west because he had heard that there were places in Bremerton, Washington, where African Americans could earn a decent salary and support their families. Soon after he arrived, my father secured a job at Puget Sound Naval Shipyard, where they repaired damaged military ships. My father loved mechanical work, and despite having only a third-grade education, he possessed a mastery of the inner workings of machinery. However, I'm unsure whether he was truly allowed to apply his knowledge. I do know that the work was hard and grueling, but honest.

When he settled, he sent for my mom and four older siblings. They, along with one of my uncles, boarded a train with no intention of looking back. With the long blast of the train's horn and a puff of smoke, they moved forward with the hope of what was to come. Not long after her arrival, my mother joined my father to punch the clock day in and day out.

**Preparing the Dream**
While the job provided well for our family, my parents felt like something was missing in their day-to-day work. It wasn't long after that that they realized they wanted more, so they decided to purchase land. They said there was pride that came from working the land with your hands to produce something of your own. They had been sweet potato farmers in Louisiana and knew what the earth could produce. Additionally, no one could take what was yours, and you would always have a source of food and a safe place for your children to come. However, before they could act on this dream, they discovered that my mother was pregnant with my sister Betty. So, they delayed the

dream until after Betty's birth. Not long after Betty's arrival, my mother discovered she was pregnant again with me. As they waited for my birth, they still dreamed and diligently saved all they could from working at the shipyard. After a two-year delay, my family found the land they had dreamed of, purchasing almost ten acres in the Highland area of Renton, Washington.

In Renton, most families worked for Boeing. They preferred the easier suburban life with a two-car garage and society meetings. Still, my family wanted this land to be their forever home. Thus, through tedious days and hard work, they cleared every piece of that land. When they finished, they stood with pride, looking over what they had accomplished. Because they had already envisioned what they wanted, the land soon bustled with pigs, cows, chickens, as well as lush vegetation.

From the rich soil, they grew juicy tomatoes, bright peppers, leafy greens — specifically, mustards and collards — yellow corn, and potatoes. They had finally found the place where they could thrive, and their children would become all they were meant to become on that land. That was the dream my parents had, and for a while, it was our reality.

After seeing my parents' success, several of my father's siblings and their families migrated to Washington state, and the Houston family's mark on the Great West was sealed. Growing up, I was never too far from a cousin or fun. Eventually, our family numbers would grow into the hundreds, but despite all they did, one thing would continue to haunt my parents and eventually become a derailing factor in our lives, and that was racism.

## Not a Part of My World

As we were growing up, my parents shared stories of growing up in Louisiana and the racism they faced. To me, racism was a completely foreign concept. They and I lived in two different worlds. I didn't understand that I thought that way because they had done such a great job protecting me. I was the baby of their children, and I was a child living free on a pig farm and adventuring in the woods. I was a Native American living off the land. I was a cowboy exploring the Great West.

I had a vivid imagination, even building a lean-to shack that resembled my version of a fort, just like the ones I saw on television or heard about through radio programs. My siblings and I played in the pond, chased frogs, picked up snakes, and did all the things one could imagine a little boy doing. Sometimes, I would stand in the woods with outstretched hands and my face to the sun, soaking in all the warmth and beauty of everything around me. The smell of the dogwood trees, pine trees, and wildflowers permeated every aspect. It was the best time of my life.

# Chapter 2
# An Idyllic Life Shattered

Being so young, I listened to but ignored the stories my parents told about their past days in Louisiana. However, within a couple of years, my idyllic life would shatter, and some of those same stories would become my reality. Racism does a dark work on a child, and how dark it becomes would rapidly manifest in the life that would lead to my downfall.

**Separate But Not Equal**
Unbeknownst to me, I was born at the height of the Civil Rights movement. By June 1953, tensions would reach a fever pitch during the Baton Rouge bus boycott. Just six months before, the Supreme Court had heard its first arguments in Brown v. Board of Education. In December 1953, they would rehear arguments. In 1954, they made their infamous ruling that separate was not equal, desegregating schools across the U.S. and giving Blacks an opportunity for a better education. I wasn't quite one year old yet, and it would be the beginning of my nightmare.

Our ten-acre farm bordered Honeydew Elementary School, where I would ultimately attend. Before I attended school, I used to watch my siblings go to school every day. From the front porch of our house, I could see my siblings and their friends playing at recess. I wanted that to be me. Yet, I was the baby of the bunch, trying to wait my turn patiently. Thus, as I held on to the wooden posts, longing to play with my friends one day at school and learn in a classroom, I scurried back inside at the sound of my mother calling my name for lunch. Since I was the only child at home during the day, I received all her love and all her care. When my dad would come in, I would follow behind him and try to do whatever he did. Later, some family members would call me Little Sam after him.

**First Day of School**
When it was finally my turn to go to school, I had an elation no one could contain. I was joining the big boy ranks, and I would do all the things my big brothers were doing. The night before my first day of school, I carefully laid out my clothes. In my mind, I had done a good job, too, until my mom came through like a drill sergeant, scrutinizing each child's attire to ensure it was appropriate. During the summer, weeks before school started, each of us had picked strawberries and beans to earn enough money to buy new clothes for school. My new clothes were worth every strawberry and bean I picked.

As my mom made a point to discuss with me the importance of appropriate behavior at school, I became a bit anxious. I had never had a teacher before, and I was not accustomed to sitting at a desk for the entire day. It seemed my mom was giving me so many instructions, like 'pay attention in class' and 'number one, no fighting.' I often roughhoused with my brothers, so I needed that instruction. As I listened, I figured I would excel at school. My brothers and sisters had seemingly mastered school, and so would I.

On the first day, I got up and immediately put on my clothes, readying myself to leave, but my mom stopped me. "Have you brushed your teeth? Have you eaten?" she asked intently. As excited as I was, I knew she was anxious to let her baby boy go. I responded that I had not brushed my teeth or eaten, so I was directed back toward the table and to the makeshift sink to brush my teeth. I did my best to eat, but I couldn't. I was bubbling with too much excitement. I did manage to brush my teeth.

As I prepared to walk out the door, my mom emphasized again, "No fighting. Listen to your teacher." Then, she scrubbed my face with her fingers because I had not cleaned it well enough. Next, she leaned in for a kiss on my face. I shrugged it off. I was joining the ranks of the big boys. Laughing, she recognized what I was doing. She adjusted my collar and jacket, then kissed me on both cheeks. I rubbed off the kisses and ran through the front door toward my first day of school.

**Anticipation**
When I arrived at the school, I burst through the doors, confident and ready. I already knew where my classroom was because my older brother and sister had shown it to me. When I walked in, my teacher asked my name and pinned a nametag on me. I happily went to my desk, ready to start my day. Even in the excitement, though, I felt something different in the air.

I didn't know quite what it was, but it was a different atmosphere. When I looked around, I noticed I was the only brown child in the classroom; however, it didn't bother me. I was at school.

When my teacher, who was white like my classmates, began to speak, I was dumbstruck by the difference in how she said certain words and how I spoke. We both spoke English, but her English was foreign compared to the southern drawl mix I had picked up at home. Despite this, I was unconcerned. I smiled as I looked at my classmates. Someone had red hair. Some wore glasses. Some were smaller, and some were bigger. There were many different types of people in my class. I wondered if they liked the same things I did, such as playing in the woods or chasing the pigs. Smiling, legs swinging, I was ready to learn and secretly looking forward to hearing the bell for recess.

**He Called Me Nigger**
Recess time finally came, and my teacher had barely permitted us to leave class before I was out of my seat. I had never sat so long. At my school, we received two recesses: one in the morning and one in the afternoon. Thus, when I was out of the classroom doors, I was ready to play. By this time, I had developed a love for sports. My dad would tell us about the Negro League and their fight to be a part of the majors, but because of racism, many of the greats had not made it to the majors. With my adventurous mind, I knew I would be among the greats, and I played like I would one day.

I was playing to my heart's content when a classmate walked up to me with his two friends alongside him. "Nigger." I looked up, confused by the term. I didn't know what it meant, but something about it felt dirty. He repeated it. "Nigger." In my mind, I wondered why he was bothering me. I wanted him to go away so I could continue playing. "Nigger." He repeated it. He finally stopped and went on to play with his friends.

Another boy from my class walked over and said, "You can play with me." This is when I made my first friend, Jimmy. It wasn't until later that I realized that some of the guys in my class had not accidentally bumped my desk multiple times and knocked my books off. Even with this realization, I still looked forward to being at school. When I met Jimmy, it was an exciting experience. He told my sister Betty and me all about his train set, and he invited us to come to his house to see it. After school, Betty and I walked a couple of miles, following him home to his modern suburban home. When we arrived, it was like I had entered a whole new world.

Jimmy had a lovely home with a double-car garage, indoor plumbing, a beautiful stove, and a jar full of cookies that his sisters had baked for him. How different it was from our outhouse and the coal and wood-lit stove my mother cooked on. After having cookies, we visited the family's garage. Jimmy's dad had installed a lift for his train set, and Jimmy could push a button to lower the train to the ground and raise it back up. My eyes remained wide for the entirety of our visit. The train set mimicked a real train, had cars that were bright orange, and covered almost the length of the garage. As Betty and I walked home, talking about everything we saw, my mother met us about a mile from the house with a belt in hand
Not coming straight home from school, she came looking for

us. Now, I know she was probably worried about other things we never imagined because we were thinking like kids, and she whipped us the whole mile back. However, the next day, I went back to Jimmy's house. It was worth the whippin' to me. It was my first adventure away from the farm.

## Confrontation

Despite receiving my whippin', I got around to telling my mom about my day. In my innocence, I said to her that my classmate had called me a nigger. My mom told me to ignore it, but the next day, she walked to the school and informed the principal that she had sent her children to school to learn, not to be afraid to go outside and play. She emphasized that it should not happen again. My brothers provided a different solution to me. I listened, but I didn't initially engage with their solution.

For two more days, the same boy and his friends would harass me, saying "Nigger" as I played quietly to myself or near Jimmy. On the third day, I had had about enough as the word continuously rolled off his tongue. I had tried it my mother's way. Now, it was time to try it my brother's way. I don't know where the power came from, but with all my might, I took my tiny fist and shoved it right into his stomach. He immediately doubled over in pain, and his friends went to tell the teacher, who was not too far from us, what had happened. I hunched my shoulders and continued to play. The next thing I knew, the looming figure of my principal approached me.

He snatched me up by my arm, saying, "Sticks and stones may break your bones, but words will never hurt you." But those words did hurt, and so did the three raps on my behind from his paddle. For the rest of the day, I had to stay in the office and miss class. As soon as I got home, I told my mom what happened. With fierce determination, she walked to the school, with me trailing behind. When she arrived, she said to the principal, with fire in her voice and demeanor, that if he ever touched me again, he would have her to deal with. She was my hero that day.

# Pictures of John Houston's family home

# Chapter 3
# Friendships and Frustrations

I wish I could say the racism stopped after my mom visited the school; nonetheless, it continued as anonymous shouts in the hall or low whispers in class. I was aware of what they were attempting to do. Despite that, a part of me fought by continuing to live life like any other kid. Thus, I focused on the good, such as when the kids would laugh and play with me when the pigs escaped from our farm and came into the schoolyard. They thought it was funny that I had to round them up and leave school to take them home. They thought it was great growing up on a pig farm, being little kids and all, but only one friend ever spent time with me at the farm. That was Mike. By the time I met Mike, I had established a solid friendship group and was happy playing with Jimmy, Dave, Rock, and Jerry. However, the night of the fire would cement what would become a lifelong friendship with Mike.

**House Fire**
I had gone to a hockey game with Jerry and his dad. We had a

great time, cheering in the stands, taunting the opposing team, and eating snacks. I didn't mind being the only Black child in the arena, as I had grown accustomed to being the only one at this point. But as we pulled up to my house after the game, all the fun and the excitement for the game disappeared. We were met by sirens and flashing lights, and I could see that my house was on fire. I'm not sure what Jerry's father said to the policeman, but he left me with them. I stood there, scared and wondering where my family was, until a lovely lady named Marlene approached me. Marlene was Mike's mom. Together, Marlene, Mike, and I watched the remainder of my house turn into ash. I didn't know Marlene, but she knew me from around the baseball field. Mike and I had played on opposing teams at one point.

Mike and Marlene lived about half a mile from our home. According to Marlene, she saw the fire from her home. When she realized the flames seemed close to our house, she told Mike she wanted to find out what was going on and how close it was to our home. So, she and Mike came to see if we were okay. When she arrived, there was nothing they could do but watch like everyone else as our home burned to the ground. It wasn't the first time someone had tried to hurt our family. Previously, someone had placed an explosive device on our porch. This time, they set fire, and because we used a lot of wood, it didn't take long for the fire to spread and consume our home. Although we had lost every physical aspect of what we owned, Marlene assured me that my family was safe and unharmed. She told the police that she would take me to my family, and she did. When I saw my family, I ran into my mother's arms, wept with joy that they were all safe, and sobbed at knowing we had lost everything.

The next day, Marlene showed up at the place where we were staying. With her were bags of clothing. For me, she had nice shirts from Nordstrom. My family could never afford anything as lovely as what she gave me. She told me that everyone should have nice things, regardless of their race, and I remember how she told Mike and me that skin color should not divide us. From then on, Mike and I were inseparable. He came to the pig farm every day. We played in the woods, shot BB guns, and got into the type of situations little boys do. Even today, we have remained friends. Back then, I wondered why his mom had chosen to help me. Later, I would learn that she understood what it felt like to be treated like an outsider. She was a Native American, once a single mother, and unaccepted by society. Then, she met her husband, who is White, and once they married, people assumed Mike was white because of his stepdad, though his actual dad was Mexican. Because of her husband, people treated Mike better. Fortunately, he didn't have to face the same backlash as I did, except when people saw him hanging out with me. Regardless, it didn't stop his loyalty. Looking back, each of my friends had played a pivotal role in my life at just the right time. I believe this was God's doing because only He could orchestrate such a bond. Often, our friendship was tested because it was the sixties, and racial unity was seen as a threat.

**The Melting Pot**
Our group's friendship was representative of what the world should look like. There was I, African-American of course, Mike, who was Native American and Mexican, and then

Jimmy, Dave, Rock, Jerry, and Steve were White. Even among my White friends, stark differences existed. Like my friend Jimmy, I met Dave on that first day of first grade. He always spoke up for me and made me laugh when others were being cruel to me. Later, we would both join the same Cub Scout Pack. As usual, I was the only Black person in the Cub Scouts. What I noticed about Dave was that he was always the same person and treated me the same, regardless of who he was around. When I was struggling with addiction during most of my adulthood, he would continue to check on my mom for me. More than fifty years later, we are still in touch with one another.

Rock was similar to Dave in that he stood for what was right, regardless of who was around. Rock had been born in Salt Lake City and raised a Mormon. Despite his quiet nature, he had the heart of a lion. One day, we decided to play basketball, and he invited me to his church because they had a gym. When we arrived, they wouldn't let me enter through the door. Rock stood in shock, confused that his place of faith would treat someone differently. That day, Rock walked away from the Mormon church. He said he couldn't have any part of a faith that would practice that type of behavior. He gave up
everything he knew to do right by me. Even in adulthood, he continued to stand with me, introducing me to his mother, which was considered a big deal. Years later, Rock succumbed to suicide after a series of difficult situations. Unfortunately, I was not there for him as he was for me due to my addiction, and today, that pain still stings.

During my junior high years, I was closest to Jerry. I met Jerry in the third grade, and we were friends from the start. This tall, redheaded White kid stood out among my friends because he listened to Motown with me and could even do a few of the Temptations' steps. Jerry came from a single-parent home and lived in the Highland Projects with his mom until she married Jerry's stepdad. When Jerry's mom married his stepdad, he moved them out of the projects to the same neighborhood as Jimmy. Both of us had strong opinions about the social issues surrounding our time. Many times, he spoke up when he heard racist terms, and sometimes, he completely removed those people using those terms from his life. He was just that type of guy. I recall that he also stood up for those with disabilities. He would catch hell from some of the bullies, but Jerry always stood firm in his beliefs.

I always felt like Jerry's home was welcoming and safe for me. Even if he were not home, his mom and dad would welcome me in for me to wait for him. Briefly, Jerry and I had to part ways in our friendship. This was during the time I started slipping into the darkness. Jerry and his parents had plans for his future, and I was not a good influence. Eventually, we mended our broken relationship, and today, he is one of my closest confidants and friends. When we were fighting for our family's land, Jerry drove hundreds of miles to testify on our behalf about the loss of our land. This guy is my brother, and our history together is deep.

As I mentioned earlier, it was Jerry's dad who took me to the hockey games. It was also Jerry's dad who let me play in my first Little League baseball game. Initially, when I tried to play baseball, I tried out for the Fraternal Order of Eagles Little

League team, but I didn't make the team. According to the coach, I wasn't good enough, so he cut me. It was clear that I was one of the most talented, but I accepted that I couldn't play and made no fuss about it. Later, I discovered that no one gets cut from Little League. Instead, they had a no Blacks policy for their team.

Despite being cut from the baseball team, I would show up every day to watch my friends play for the VFW (Veterans of Foreign War) Little League team. One day, Jerry's dad, who was the coach, asked me why I wasn't playing. When I told him what the other coach said—that I wasn't good enough—he told me to come to practice the next day. The next day, I was on the VFW team. I scored the first baseman position and served as a cleanup hitter. I was so excited. A couple of years later, I was playing first base for one of the best Pony League teams in the state.

Later, we had another guy join our group, Steve. I met Steve in my first year of high school and his last year of junior high. Like us, he also loved sports. The difference between Steve and my other friends was that his family was like my family, except they were White. All my other friends' fathers worked for Boeing, but Steve understood the economic bottom like I did. Our parents were similar in that they didn't concern themselves with our whereabouts, expecting us always to do the right thing. Yet, Steve and I, along with a mutual acquaintance, indulge in things teenage boys snuck to do back then: a little beer drinking and marijuana smoking. We had great times, although we shouldn't have done the things we did. Often, others picked on Steve, calling him names not because of his economic status but because he hung out with me. I found myself defending Steve, and he defended me in return. To this day, we both acknowledge the importance of our friendship to one another.

Together, Jimmy, Dave, Larry, Jerry, Rock, Mike, Steve, and I would accomplish some incredible things in sports and beyond. They were the strength I needed when I faced some of my toughest challenges from elementary through high school. For example, I remember when I was finally able to wear my VFW uniform; I was so proud. It was Saturday morning, game day. I strutted down the street in my crisp, red, and white VFW uniform, my glove in hand, which I purchased by picking beans. Oiling it myself, I worked hard to mold it into the proper shape for my hand. Also, my mom had found a used jockstrap at the thrift store, so I had every essential item that my other teammates had. On my way to the game, a car full of men pulled alongside me and said, "Look at the little nigger in a monkey suit." I was stunned, frightened, and saddened. When would it stop? Yet, when I arrived at the game, the guys treated me like a brother. This was part of my saving grace.

**Pressure**
Over time, I became utterly immersed in the White world, listening to the Beatles and even wearing the Beatles' boots. As I did, I learned how to shift between the two worlds. At home, I spoke the southern dialect my parents articulated, and outside the house, I learned to communicate in a way that White society was pleased to hear me speak. I dated primarily White girls, even though this caused quite a bit of controversy in our community. Yet, there were only about five Black

families in the community. Choices were limited. Only two of the girls from Black families caught my attention, but as our sports acumen grew as a group, so did my choices in women. I found White girls to be very sympathetic to my plight as a Black teen who was constantly bullied. In all of this, I was losing myself without even realizing it.

Before high school, it was evident that our core friend group had an exceptional talent for sports. We played everything together: baseball, basketball, and football, regardless of the weather outside. This garnered a great deal of attention for our group. In sixth grade, we were good. In junior high, I stood out as an outstanding player. When we reached high school, basketball was the sport of choice, though my father preferred baseball. We faced a lot of racist pressure because I was among them, and it was affecting some of my friends more than me, because they wanted to be accepted by their society. It's a strange feeling when your people reject you. I was disheartened when I learned that some of my friends had started to exclude me from sleepovers, camping, and other activities because of the racist who invited them. Either they wouldn't tell me about events so they would not have to explain, or they pretended they were doing something else as a cover for their real activities. No longer naïve, mistrust started to invade my thoughts, but my friends were all I knew. Mike and Rock remained the same, refusing to give in to the pressure. For a while, I endured the pain, knowing what they were doing, but eventually, I became angry due to the hurt. I couldn't keep pretending. I was trying to fight racism with assimilation and my fist, and I was losing the war. All I wanted was these people's respect. Why couldn't they respect me like everyone realize then is that I didn't need their respect as long as I respected myself.

John Houston (in red) sitting on his father's lap alongside his siblings

# Chapter 4
# The Breaking

While certain friendships were deteriorating, I faced another deterioration in my life, my family falling apart. I had a sense that something was happening, but I didn't know exactly what it was. Like a snake, it slithered its way in, ripping us apart. After the fire, my parents rebuilt our home, but in the years that followed, something had gone wrong along the way.
Previously united in their dreams of success, they grew to a point where one parent wanted to protect the family and move to another city to start over. In contrast, the other wanted to stand their ground and continue the fight. I didn't understand how bad it was until I came home one day from school and walked in on my parents, ferociously arguing. I had never seen them like this before. I felt so overwhelmed that I screamed and walked out of the house. The final straw had been laid. They tried to get rid of us by intimidation, burning our house down, and measly buyout proposals. Through it all, my family stood, but now, they had found a new way to kill my family's dream: eminent domain.

## Eminent Domain

As poor as we were, we were rich in land. It seemed everyone around us could see the potential of what we had or what could happen if we decided to sell one day. It began with the Renton School District stating that they needed a new school and deciding that our land was the perfect spot. When a city has a need, it can utilize eminent domain to fulfill that need, as long as it offers those it is encroaching upon a fair price. But then, they weren't offering Blacks fair prices on anything. I learned a lot by watching my father run his business. White people would pay one price for his offerings but pay a higher price for the same offer of lesser quality from someone else, keeping us economically disadvantaged and reminding us once again of our place.

Being one of the largest, if not the largest, landowners in the area, we were an easy target. Even with her seventh-grade education, my mother knew what the school district was up to. She had cleaned for a lawyer and wanted to fight the school district. My father was tired and ready to create a new dream. He had a new plan, Moses Lake! My mom pleaded with him to stay. She didn't want to uproot us from everything we knew and loved. I was only four years away from graduating from high school, but my father's heart was broken. He knew they would take it whether he chose to give it to them or not. So, the city had him sign an X for his name, and that was the end of our family's dream and the end of our family. My parents divorced. My father moved to Moses Lake with a new girlfriend, and my mother kept Betty and me behind to finish school. I was fourteen years old.

They never did build a school on our land. Eventually, they would sell it to a developer and build homes that my family could never afford to live in. I walked by our land every day, knowing we would never get it back. Though it was scary, my mother bought a new home in a relatively nice neighborhood. Life was comfortable. It wasn't Jimmy's house, but it wasn't the farm either. Mom went back to school, taking classes to become a home health nurse. I was so proud of how well she did. Soon after she finished, she was hired by a health clinic. As painful as it was losing our land and losing her husband, my mom had fought through it all. I'm sure we were a motivating factor to keep going; however, I wasn't doing as well.

Something had broken in me, losing my beloved woods, my place of serenity, the land, and my father, whom I rarely saw after that. Though he would never have admitted it, it broke his heart to remain in the place that took everything that mattered to him. Sometimes, when I played baseball, I would catch glimpses of him in the parking lot. He would drive several hours just to look in, but by the time I arrived at the parking lot to say hello after the game, he was gone. He would receive most of his news about me through his brother. I was not coping well, and I had more free time. Thus, I found myself experimenting with more trouble while my mom was busy in school and securing a new job. I would attend school, practice after school, and then do whatever mischief my friends and I had planned for the day. By the time my mom got home, everything seemed to be in order. I had learned a long time ago to live in two worlds and present two different realities. I was out of control.

## When the Cheers Stopped

Basketball remained my favorite sport, and I had the opportunity to play on both the junior varsity and varsity teams at Hazen High School. I excelled. The more I excelled, the more popular I became, and the more popular I became, the more aware I became that they did not want me there. I would show up. I would work extra hard and smile. I would do everything they told me to do while living in total misery. To this day, I don't understand how I was as productive as I was on the court when I was drinking and drugging regularly. Unfortunately, for the people who did know what was happening behind the scenes, no one made any effort to stop me. I was good, and they needed good. Thus, I was the stereotypical jock and stoner.

Despite my destructive behavior, I had dreams of going further —college—and I knew basketball was the venue that would whisk me away to a better life—a life where I would feel respected. During basketball season, I lived off the emotional high of being a great player and local fame. After the games, alcohol flowed, and drugs were supplied in abundance. While I was on the court, even the racists cheered, but the problems came when the season was over. People who had cheered for me wouldn't even look at me without a ball in my hand after the season was over, and they had no problem reminding me of my place. That push and pull on my emotions was mimicking the addiction that was forming. They just wouldn't let me be great. I needed the high to remind me that I could still dream.

## Champion and Failure

My senior year was the culmination of all the hard work I had put into sports. The previous year, the coaches had discovered the right combination for a winning team. One other Black guy, I, and some of my friends were on the team heading toward the championship. What made us great was the oneness of mind we had as a team. No one player treated the other as if they were less than. This allowed us to play with the fervor necessary to take it to the next level. In addition to this winning mentality, my Black teammate and I had a pact. We pushed each other with intensity. Because people often saw us as one, we would never leave a game without one of us, if not both of us, being on top. Thus, if he fell behind in double-digit shooting, I would pick up the slack, and if I fell behind in double-digit shooting, he would pick up the slack. We created a rhythm. We had a drive. We wanted better. Yet, after every game, it was the same for me. We celebrated, the alcohol flowed, and drugs were in abundance. This was my continuous high.

Eventually, our basketball success led to our advancing to the regional playoffs and being featured in top newspapers. People were asking, "Who is this unknown high school making noise?" We were making the noise, and I loved every ounce of it. No one could believe we had made it to the state championship. I remember my mom telling me how proud she was of me. I felt so good. Although I was a big boy, I still needed that love from my mom.

Being declared the best team in Western Washington, I knew game day would be epic. Before game day, they made sure we were celebrated to the utmost. In those moments, I felt whole, one with my counterparts, and of course, they supplied us with

John Houston making the shot
Photo provided by Linda Wanless

the highs we needed. I don't know how I even got out of bed on the day of the championship, considering all the partying we did, but I did. All morning, our phone rang with congratulations, too many to count and too many to acknowledge. We were on top of the world!

## The Final Buzzer

As I stood on the court, the lights were bright, and the bleachers were filled. This championship game was everything my friends and I had worked so hard for, practicing rain or shine. I remembered my makeshift basketball goal, a piece of wood nailed to a tree, and all the dreams I had. Now, I was here. Now, I would be a champion. The referee blew his whistle, and the hustle was on. Immediately, my Black friend and I established our rhythm. He signaled his next move. I signaled mine. We drove that ball down the court like everything in life depended on what we were doing. The cheers and shouts thundered in our ears while we did our best to concentrate. The opposition didn't even faze me. One shot. Two shots. Three shots. We were at the state championship, baby! We gave it all on that court, but when the final whistle blew, we were short and lost the state championship. Still, it was a performance of a lifetime. My mom smiled so much, and despite the loss, we partied and had a great time! I soaked it all in. I had had my choice of women and anything else I wanted, but unbeknownst to me, that would be my last actual official school basketball game.

For days after the state championship, people asked me which college I was attending. With my performance, everyone knew I had scholarship offers. Though I had planned for basketball to save me, it was strange that I had not heard from anyone about college. I thought they were waiting to let me know my choices. Then, I ran into a coach from Bellevue Community College. He told me he had spoken to my coach about me attending. My coach had never mentioned the offer to me, and I wondered how many other undiscussed offers might be on the table. By the time I found out why, it was too late. I wasn't eligible to graduate from high school. I was confused. I know I didn't have the best grades, but I was doing everything else that all the other athletes were doing. That was the unspoken plan. According to the counselor, I was one math credit short. Technically, I was not eligible to play basketball, but I did play, all the way to the state championship. No one ever said anything. They had used me for their purposes and discarded my future in the process. The darkness consumed me.

# SECTION II
# BLOCKING
# THE SUNLIGHT

# Chapter 5
# Caught Up in the Cycle

Anger consumed me. The emotional overwhelm I felt was unlike anything I had experienced before. Now, I understood why my father's heart was broken. What they had done to him, they had done to me differently. Though he had tried to reclaim his dream by starting over, he never reached the pinnacle he once achieved, and at eighteen years old, I received the phone call that plummeted me. My mother wailed as she told me my father had died. Though he had left us behind, she still loved him and believed in him. Between being stripped of my dream and my father's death, the world just seemed like a ravenous monster with only the intent to kill. I spiraled out of control, and the journey to my thirty-six-year addiction was in full swing.

**Shattered Dreams and Jealousy**
I did have a chance to start over before I completely spiraled out of control. I had remained in touch with the Bellevue basketball coach, who extended an invitation to participate in

a summer league. I played well enough for the coach to offer me a scholarship, provided I completed the one math credit to graduate during the first quarter. I didn't complete the math credit. I quit, left school after that first quarter. I was so lost, searching for a role model who could help me find myself and see myself as someone worth fighting for. With my father gone, my older brother was the best thing to have as a father figure, but my naivety about who he truly was as a person left me unprotected and vulnerable. What I realized much later in life is that you must be around people who are going where you want to go.

My brother, with his shattered dreams and jealous demeanor, was not seeking my best interest. Being years apart, I had the opportunity to go further in high school and gain more notoriety. Yet, he and some other family members struggled with the success I had, calling me "Uncle Tom," the derogatory slang used for Black people who were Black on the outside but considered White on the inside. I wasn't Black enough. I wasn't White enough. Where did I fit? My father was gone. I was no longer little Sam. I had some friends abandon me. I wasn't good enough for this person or that person. Why was I even here? I didn't think their attitude was damaging at the time, but the mentality laid the groundwork for introducing me to crack cocaine.

The first time I tried crack cocaine, I was with my brother. From the moment I took my first hit, I knew crack cocaine was going to change my life. Instantly, my brain experienced euphoria. I felt no pain, no sadness, and no care. Like the street name for it, "White girl", it seduced me to new heights. I didn't need anything else. I was good. I was happy. I was at peace until the high wore off. When the high wore off, I wanted more. My pusher happily obliged, and I floated into a place where I felt like no one could hurt me, and I wanted to stay there.

## Glimpses of Fading Hope

Despite my drug use, a particular ambition lay within me. In many ways, my father's character as a man is reflected in me. Known as a jack-of-all-trades, he wasn't just a farmer. He owned a wrecking company and a metal stripping company, and he took on various odd jobs to support his family. The difference was that I was just ambitious enough to support my habit. As I became more hooked on crack cocaine, my habit became more expensive. I worked two jobs to support my habit. At the time, my mother was not aware of the extent of my addiction and recognized an opportunity to introduce me to home ownership due to my hard work. I loved the idea of home ownership. Maybe, I could recapture some of the things my family had lost.

One day, I mentioned the idea of home ownership to my friend, Rock, and we decided that we would both buy houses in the same neighborhood, wait two years, and then sell for a profit. I was so happy the day we found our houses. At only nineteen years old, I was a homeowner. Rock and I had done exactly what we said. I worked. I lived in my home for two years, then sold it for a hefty profit of $5,000, which is equivalent to just over $15,000 in today's market. I could have taken the money and reinvested in more properties, started a business, gone to school, or achieved many of the other ambitions that were drifting inside me. Instead, that crack cocaine gripped me, and I tottered between wanting to live in this world's reality and my mind's fantasy. Without an adequate coping mechanism in place, I slipped further into the abyss of my addiction, and just like that, all the money I had made from my home sale was gone.

**Smacked with Reality**
Like a racer, I was living life fast and hot. Besides my drug use, I had a few different women I was seeing. I suppose I thought I was somebody for a little while, at least. Maybe it was reminiscent of my glory days, when people chanted my name. These women also fueled the euphoria, each serving a distinct purpose. When I would introduce the women to my mother, she would often make a mean face toward them, which scared most of them off. Looking back, that was a good thing because I could only imagine how much more out of control my life would have been. Among those my mother liked was my now ex-wife, Helen. Helen was of mixed ancestry, with a dark-skinned Indonesian father and a Dutch mother. I instantly fell in love with her mother for taking a stand and marrying the man she loved. Ironically, her father didn't want her to date a Black man, though he was nearly as dark as I. Maybe it was because he understood the hardships she would face.

After high school, Helen and her family moved to California, and although we had remained friendly with one another, I hadn't seen her in a while, as I had a rotating array of women. Nevertheless, mine and Helen's fate would become permanently intertwined after a visit to California. My problems with my brother had continued to escalate as we both ventured further into the drug world. Situations were becoming alarmingly violent; robberies were becoming more common around us. My brother had expanded his user list to include girls I like. He had become so ingrained in the criminal world that I found myself standing close to death. I had to get out of Washington for a while, and under the guise of vacationing with a girl I liked at the time, I visited California.

When we arrived in California, I left my then-girlfriend in the hotel room and paid a visit to Helen. I was not the man I wanted to be. Drugs had taken me to an unexpected low. When I saw her, she was still as beautiful as ever. Having always been a sweet and caring person, I felt like I had fallen in love with her all over again. That night, our first child was conceived. I returned to Washington with my then-girlfriend, only for my madness to continue. I swung between being a good guy people loved to one who was always on the brink of danger. Eventually, I hooked up with prostitutes, who loved me for my protective nature, but at the same time bought into the lie that I would somehow grow into something more. I didn't need to work; I just needed to be there for them, and from that alone, I made thousands of dollars. However, Helen's phone call changed everything. She was pregnant. I wanted to do the right thing. I moved to California, I married Helen, and I stood in the room as my first daughter was born. As I held her for the first time, I cried. I would never leave this beautiful little one.

John Houston with his daughters
Photo provided by Helen Stevens

# Chapter 6
# I Lost It All

Holding my daughter in my hand felt unreal, and from the instant I saw her, she was the apple of my eye. Determined to be a good father, I built the American dream. We had a lovely home. Helen naturally assumed the roles of both wife and mother. I had a good job. Everything was beautiful. This was the life I wanted, but still having not dealt with the demon in my life, I could not sustain it. Soon, that master came calling again. Yet this time, I invited trouble to skirt near my home.

**Same Scenarios, Different People**
It is easy to give in to pressure when things are going wrong. I think someone forgot to tell me that it is just as easy to give in to pressure when things are going right, too. It is puzzling. As men, we often question whether we can fulfill our jobs well and truly meet all the responsibilities expected of a husband and a father. Helen did everything to make our marriage work. Still, societal pressure, uncertainty about the future, and constant worry about my safety and financial stability, due to

continuous disrespect in various places, prevented me from holding onto the good.

I looked at my wife, who had the opportunity to work in a bank, and I loved the respect she received when she walked in, as well as how they greeted her. Though people liked my personality, I could always tell the difference. While the difference in treatment was very real, I now understand that I was also dealing with post-traumatic stress. Back then, Black culture and psychology were taboo subjects. So, though I had everything I needed in my world, I self-sabotaged, searching for my master and found her in the arms of the local gangs. My disease had progressed.

**In and Out**
Inside me, I had an invisible boundary. I did not want to be a part of the local gangs. I wanted what they had. I could leave my house and cross over to the other side of town, have what I needed in less than ten minutes, and be back home in less than twenty. They loved me and greeted me as if I were a brother. There was no question about whether I was Black enough or if I leaned toward White attributes. They loved and respected me for what I could invest in their street enterprise. In return, they demanded that people respect me. Thus, what came along with my investment in their enterprise was extra protection, and because I was in their volatile world where situations shifted quickly, I needed them.

Robberies, the needy taking from the already impoverished, were standard in California, as it was in Washington. On two occasions, I was robbed while returning from obtaining my purchase. The first time, I didn't take action. The second time, I went home, grabbed a stick from my closet, and came back to hit the guy from behind. He was much bigger than I. Regardless, I did not care. I was over being disrespected. Then, I informed the gang members, and they took care of the situation. My life was night and day. During the daytime, I was the smiling, friendly worker. At night, I became like the darkness that consumed me. Many did not see the evidence, but my wife, Helen, knew.

**Broken Promises**
At home, where no one could see, I was a threat. I took money from my wife's purse without her knowing it, and then dared her to question me about it. Over time, we reached a point where I boldly took what I wanted, and she cowered under my demands. No more hiding. Despite all the signs, she still believed in me. She believed in my promises. At the time, I meant what I said about getting better and maintaining a good lifestyle; nevertheless, it only lasted as long as I could stay away from my next high. I knew I was making mistakes, and whether I realized it then or not, everything was slowly slipping away from me. I kept leaning on the grace of my wife and those, like my mother, who were praying for me.

As the drugs emboldened me, I started bouncing between jobs. I was a great worker until I was not. The two jobs that continuously offered me security were my work as a produce clerk and office machine technician. As the doors of opportunity closed with various companies and my family life deteriorated to an unrecognizable state, I started to realize I needed help. Helen was pregnant again, and I needed to get just enough help to keep my job secure and not destroy my family life. I went to my union and requested drug recovery treatment.

**First Attempt**
I was thrilled when I received the news that I had been accepted into Azure Acres' twenty-eight-day treatment program. Two hours north of San Francisco, this beautiful facility was a former hunting lodge, featuring forty rooms, a swimming pool, a fireplace, and tennis courts. It sat on five acres of gorgeous green land and featured an apple orchard and a vineyard, which produced the finest wines in Napa Valley. I was fortunate that the union chose to pay for the $14,000 treatment. For twenty-eight days, I listened, I bonded, and I did everything I was supposed to do. I wanted to make it through, to pull my life back together, to please them and win them back. Even many of the people I met at the facility, including the wealthy, shared my attitude. Needless to say, I had already set myself up to fail again.

While I was at the facility, I heard stories of families being torn apart by drugs and loved ones dying. I listened, yet like a fast train entering a tunnel, the stories briefly filled my ears and dissipated as soon as the darkness seemed to be gone. I was not affected. No doubt existed that the information was valuable; I was not ready to apply it. Like I had learned as a child, I spoke the words they wanted to hear, and it seemed I was the ideal patient. I appeared better, and I was happy when they allowed my wife and daughter to visit me. Despite all my antics, I missed them, and they missed me. Like I did for the counselors, I put on a great show. They were happy that I was doing so much better. When I was finally released to go home, I knew what to do, but I was not disciplined enough to do it. What I learned most was how to deceive people into thinking I was better.

**Second Attempt**
Like I had been a practicing addict, I needed to practice what they taught at Azure Acres. Because I knew this was what they wanted to see, I went to a few twelve-step meetings after returning home. I made a greater effort at home, worked on my marriage, and excelled as a star employee. Yet, relapse was near. Slowly, I made excuses for not attending twelve-step meetings. It was not the people. They were friendly and very welcoming. Slowly, the pressure crept back in. I needed to relax, and like all addictions, she called to me, and I answered.

At this point, I had been sober for two months. I thought that if I only sprinkled a little crack in my cigarette, I would be okay. However, the joke was on me, and my master fully reawakened. Again came the lies to Helen and others I cared about. For my fix, I became entangled with the gang again. When I first approached them after rehab, they were suspicious because they had not seen me in a while. I lied and told them that I had to go to Seattle to attend to family business. When I said that and rolled out money, the tension in the air released. Things were like they used to be, except worse.

My craving came back with a vengeance. I wanted the crack cocaine even more. Though my need was heightened, I managed to present a grand façade at work for a while. At home, where no one could see me, the fear returned for my family. I was even violent. I knew that what I was doing would eventually catch up with me, but I could not stop myself. I started using crack cocaine every day. I became nervous and agitated. I started creating situations with Helen, which gave me reasons to leave the house for a few hours.

I know my manager knew. Under the guise that they needed me to work at another store, they transferred me. Later, I would find out it was because my manager no longer wanted me at his store. I could not lose my job. Helen was close to giving birth to our second child. At this point, Helen, like my mom, had turned me over to God to deal with me. In the midst of my trying to figure out what to do, Helen went into early labor, and my daughter Renee was born on Valentine's Day.

## Who Should We Save?

During her pregnancy, Helen had developed toxemia and was experiencing life-threatening high blood pressure. I remember the doctor trying to explain the situation to me. I leaned against the wall in a fog, as he told me that I needed to choose who would live, because they didn't know if both could make it. As I laid my face in my hands, I made one of the toughest decisions I had to make, and I was not in the right mindset to make it. I chose for them to save my wife. My mind was perplexed as to how something as beautiful as childbirth could suddenly turn tragic. However, I didn't know the baby; I knew my wife, and I chose to be with someone I was familiar with. That incident alone should have been enough to prompt a change in my lifestyle. By God's grace, both Helen and Renee survived. When they allowed me to, I held and rocked Renee in my arms until the nurses took her away.

Briefly, we were a happy family again. My mother was ecstatic at the birth of her second granddaughter, and we chose Rachel as our new baby's middle name. With the trauma behind us, Helen and I planned to move forward. I tried to be worthy of being my mother's son, to be a good husband and father, but I could not on my own. I needed to go back to treatment. When I told my mother I needed to go back into treatment, she wailed the same way she had wailed when my father died. She said, "You are not an addict." Yet, I was. I believe she wanted the power of those words to take root in me somehow, but I needed more than words. I know she had seen me do incredible things while I was in high school on the basketball court, buying my first home at nineteen, and even settling down and starting a family, but her son was an addict. I reached back out to the union, and they chose to provide me one more round of twenty-eight-day treatment. I was grateful.

When I decided to go back into treatment, Helen was already tired. I went in for treatment, completed the twenty-eight-day program, and came home. My thinking and behavior were the same. As it had progressed before, my behavior worsened, but this time around, I became involved with another woman. Helen and I had two children to support, and for her, that was enough to leave and move back in with her parents. She went and briefly started a new life, even dating a guy from her job. I wanted my family back, and I did whatever it took to reunite with them. So, we tried again.

Not long afterward, I was back to my usual antics, and my behavior worsened. I don't have a reason why, other than the drugs, but I cheated on Helen again. I was fired from my new job after hitting another car with the company car and failing to meet the victim's demands. I got another job with a company I had previously worked for. I cheated on Helen again with a woman I worked with, which turned into a full-blown affair. One day, when I came home, Helen and our two daughters, Marisa and Renee, were gone.

**It Was Over**
Initially, I wasn't worried that they weren't at home. Maybe, they went out to run errands, but usually when I pulled up to the driveway, the girls would be outside playing and greet me with a smile and a hug, running and toddling into my arms. Helen would have dinner prepared, and I would make the girls laugh with my elaborate stories. But no one was playing in the driveway, and no food sat on the stove ready to be served for dinner. After a few hours had passed, I called my in-laws, hoping the girls might still be at their grandparents' house.

When my mother-in-law answered the phone, I could immediately tell something was wrong. She was not mean, but stated that her daughter and grandchildren had given up on me and needed to get some help. Helen had taken the girls to a women's shelter. The location was undisclosed, allowing them to receive the help they required safely and anonymously. Though my drug addiction had led me to this point, I was angry with the world and blamed everyone else for what happened. For days, I wavered between being angry at those I loved and figuring out some way to get revenge. Amid this psychological rampage, I had people in and out of my house, doing whatever. I lost my father's shotgun to theft because I left these people in my house while I was gone. When I came home, the house was filthy, and I sat among the filth, still trying to figure out what to do. My mother was heartbroken. Then, reality sank in. There was no getting them back. My time in California had ended. It was time to return to Washington.

Before I left California, I had one request. I wanted to say goodbye to Helen and my children, but it didn't happen. On the day I left, I only had the contents of the moving truck with me. I was broken, lonely, and pathetic. With the money from my retirement account and my last paycheck, I set off. On my way home to Renton, I stopped in Sacramento to buy crack. Alone in my hotel room, I did not sleep. I let the crack and alcohol take me away from the pain. At the same time, I pleaded with God to take the addiction from me. He didn't. The next morning, I got up and finished the drive to Renton. I arrived at my mother's doorstep defeated, and life was set to get worse before it got better.

> "My worlds continued to collide, creating destruction."

# Chapter 7
# Losing Marques

When I arrived at my mom's home, she didn't tolerate my pity party and strongly suggested that I find a job. She didn't have to encourage me much because my brothers and sisters' irritation with me living at home again motivated me to prove I could succeed. I was determined to reunite with my family. Not long afterward, I found a new job, and the atmosphere was completely different.

Every day, I worked alongside professionals, and I had a clear career path ahead of me. I was motivated, and I used crack a little less every day. However, as the pressure of managing success mounted, I found myself struggling again. The pressures were mostly self-imposed. I had to pretend that I was doing well and not using. I felt most pressured not to hurt my mother, Helen, Marisa, and Renee again. Pretend as I might, I could not sustain not using drugs. I flipped that switch on, and my mother saw firsthand how devastating my actions were.

## Just the Two of Us

While I lived in Renton, my relationship with my now ex-wife, Helen, and the children improved. Although Helen was not willing to take me back, she allowed me to talk to my daughters any time I wanted. I was thankful for this small grace. By this time, my oldest daughter, Marisa, was ten years old, and she expressed her desire to come live with me and her grandmother. I was taken aback. The bond I had formed with her early on remained, and I was surprised when her mother agreed to it. The day she walked off the plane into my arms, I cried. My addiction had caused my child to choose where she wanted to live. She should have had her whole family with her. But alas, I could not go back, and I welcomed her with open arms.

Having my oldest daughter with me forced me to think more responsibly. I stopped much of my illegal behavior. I met someone at my job and started dating. Everything was going so well that I was able to move out of my mother's home and obtain an apartment for my daughter and me two blocks from where I grew up. My daughter loved my new girlfriend. She was getting to know the African-American side of her family, and she was thriving. While she thrived, I did better. I felt like someone again. I loved having the responsibility, but it came to a screeching halt with a letter from California. My daughter was to return to the custodial parent. I was hurt, but I did not fight it. It was what was best. While I was being more responsible than I had been before, that demon continued to lurk in the background. I would have moments where I was not sober, not as many as before, but with a child, you cannot risk one moment of not being sober-minded.

When Helen and her father arrived to take Marisa back to California, I clung to her as long as I could before letting go. I knew it was right that she was leaving, but my insides screamed that if I could choose to cling to what was most important versus my addiction, life would be what it needed to be. Yet, I was not ready to tame that demon, and my daughter left my life. I fully delved into what I knew once again.

I struggled with what had happened. I couldn't face my mother, so I ran and moved to Tacoma to live with my sister. With her being an addict too, we cooked up a recipe for violence. My move there did not last long. She kicked me out, and I moved back to Bremerton, where my parents first started their dream. While in Bremerton, I discovered that I was fighting glaucoma and required emergency surgery. Though I was close to going completely blind, my addiction continued to lead me into poor decision-making.

**A Legacy Skewed**
My worlds continued to collide, creating destruction. As I was dealing with my vision diagnosis, I met the woman who would become the mother of my first son. She was a drug dealer with two children, and I was me. I did not care what she did, as long as I had what I wanted. However, before meeting her, she was facing jail time due to an assault charge. When the conviction was secured, she went away, except that our situation was a bit more complicated. She was pregnant with my child, and she still had two children at home. I wanted to make it work, so I took on the responsibility of her two children, taking them to see their mother while she served time, and later moving in with her mother and stepfather, who helped during the later

stages of pregnancy.

The day my son was born felt like a new opportunity to get it right. After the c-section, they let me hold him and rock him. He was such a healthy child, I instantly thought, "Yes! A basketball player!" I named him after my favorite Hall of Fame basketball player, Marques Johnson. In my mind, Marques Houston would set the world ablaze with his talents and abilities, but she chose a different last name, the last name of her other children. She had decided that she wanted them to all have the same last name, the last name of her previous children's father, who had been killed due to his gang ties. There would be no Marques Wayne Houston to carry on my legacy. This broke something in me; I couldn't stay, and our relationship came to an end. I returned to my mother's, and they moved to Tacoma.

**He Was His Father**
I had never planned to return to Tacoma because the drug scene was rougher than Renton, but for my son's sake, I made efforts to visit him. I knew how it felt when my dad was not there. By the time I returned to see him, his mother had a new boyfriend, and my son was calling him Dad, though he knew I was his biological father. By the age of five, he stated as much, reminding me that I was only his biological father. It was the man who was there every day who felt like his real father. Now, not only did he not have my last name, but another man had the honor of being called Dad. It was not right, but I was not right enough to change the situation appropriately.

I don't know if I thought we could rekindle our relationship or if it was some form of revenge, but when she called me, we would sneak and have relations while her boyfriend was at work. This happened a few times until something inside me would not let me continue the behavior. Even with this moral decision, I was still not who I needed to be, quickly slipping back into old affiliations and habits. This time around, I found myself in deeper trouble. Now, I had an assault charge and had to complete jail time in Pierce County. When I got out, I went back to Bremerton.

> "I cried, but my tears were not heavy enough."

# Chapter 8
# Losing Isaiah

When I returned to Bremerton, it was more of the same. The cycle continued, worsening slightly with each passing year. I would get a job, find a place to live, have a woman, lose a job, and start over again. In between the chaos, I had sporadic visits with my daughter, Marisa, with whom I always did my best to stay sober around, but ultimately, divine intervention could only be my savior. For another ten years, my life would consistently spiral despite my mother's continuous prayers and others sharing how they believed in me. Although I couldn't fully understand what they were doing for me at the time, I needed it because I had a strong desire to keep trying, despite my repeated failures.

**Dee**
During this time, I met a woman named Dee, a beautiful, outgoing, and intelligent black woman. When I first saw her, I knew she was someone I wanted to get to know. She was my

Delilah to my Samson. Her charm took all my strength. Our relationship was both intoxicating and toxic, and I couldn't get enough. Like me, she had both succeeded and failed at life. Once a registered nurse, her life had diminished to that of a drug-addicted prostitute, but I wouldn't discover that until much later. In my drug-driven mind, we could shake this drug world together and have a good life. My mother and some in my family even liked her, but they did not know then what our lives would consist of when the sun set. There was so much goodness in her if only she made the right decisions to let that goodness out. Yet, she survived based on how well she treated a man, and ultimately, I was another victim in her sight.

Though I eventually figured out that she only wanted me for my social security check and the temporary comfort I could give her, I would let her pull me in every time. When she disappeared after the money and drugs were gone, I didn't even care, as long as she came back to me. Honestly, the way she came and went, I felt it was payback for all the women I had wronged in the past. We fed each other's perplexed cycles, and despite the crazy dynamics of our relationship, we did try to stick together.

For years, Dee and I lived together on and off. Often, we were homeless because crack cocaine saw our money before the rent. Well, technically, I was often homeless. She would always find a place to stay with a female friend or a drug dealer. On numerous occasions, I went to bust her out of those drug dealers' houses. Invariably, a physical altercation ensued. In my mind, I guess I was showing strength, while she felt it was like a game. In reality, I was a weak shadow, the type of man I had always despised. And Dee, she played us all, and I continued to call what we had a relationship.

There were times when my life was in danger because of what she said. She would lie to gang members and drug dealers, saying I had beaten her up and taken her dope and money. I was threatened several times by people who used her for sex. Some people would buy into her lies and hide her from me. When I was back on my feet and thriving again, she would return, and I accepted her back every time. I know this was not normal; this was the effect of the drug use. I couldn't make rational decisions, despite being able to see the detrimental nature of the problem. She was like that crack, taking me on the wildest ride of my life. At one point, I questioned how I went from getting high for fun to making the drug life my full-time job.

**Moments of Clarity**
Sometimes, as I sat in parks or the alleys behind clubs when I had no place to stay, I would have these brief moments of clarity. In my dirty and despicable state, contrasting visions of what had been or what I could have had would flash in my mind. I thought about my life with my now-ex-wife and daughters. I remember my ex-wife's home-cooked meals, the way she dressed, how she carried herself, and how people respected her. I thought about how my girls laughed as I told them stories and how they loved when I picked them up and swung them around. I thought about how much my mother prayed for me, believing I could still be something better than I was. The corners of my mouth would slightly curl into a somewhat crooked smile. Then, my thoughts were interrupted

as someone drove down the alley looking for drugs, and I was off like a dog chasing a fox.

I knew what I was doing, what I had become, but a part of me still denied my reality. The crack had me thinking I looked good, cool, at times when I hadn't taken a bath in days. Even when I saw women clutching their purses around me or heard the car door lock at intersections, I was in full-blown denial about who I had chosen to be. People feared me. I was a junkie. Nevertheless, God kept sending me people who tried to get me to live in those moments of clarity.

**Nick and Randy**
Nick and Randy were both from India and owned convenience stores in the neighborhoods I roamed in. They both knew I did drugs; however, they never felt threatened by me like others. Nick would allow me to complete odd jobs for him, even letting me behind the counter at times. He would give me food to ensure I was eating because, honestly, I was living off of drugs more than anything. I was even around his wife and kids. He was so kind to me, and I never stole from him or became a threat. I think Nick's actions were his way of trying to help me get my head together. It was almost as if he could see something in me that I never could see in myself.

Randy showed the same trust as Nick. He would tell me, "Take what you want on credit," and interestingly, I would always pay him back. Like Nick, he saw something in me, and I was always happy to help him out when I could. Due to their nationality, people would sometimes harass the clerks. One day, Randy asked if I could help him out by hanging around as a sort of security to keep the harassment down. I did, and that kept situations under control for the most part. There was one incident when some of my drinking buddies came in and stole from Randy's. I had no idea what they had done. The next day, I went into the store, and the clerk pointed me out as one of the thieves. Randy said, "His name is Johnny, and Johnny does not steal. If Johnny needs anything and I'm not here, let him have it. Johnny always pays, and he never steals." In those moments, life was sweet, even if I was a junkie. I felt I could have moved forward if I continued to stay around them, but when Dee reentered my world, chaos once again ensued.

**Isaiah**
When Dee came back, our toxic cycle would restart. We often wandered the streets of Kitsap County, walking beyond Bremerton to get what we needed. We had an unspoken system where we worked together if required, and at other times, we worked alone to hustle enough to get drug money or drugs. We were both skilled at what we were doing. So, the day she told me she was pregnant, I was shocked. Dee had had five children who were all taken by the state due to her drug use and ultimately adopted out. Though I could not be sure if the child were mine, and we were not in a state to care for a baby, I could not bring myself to say get an abortion. Despite knowing what we faced, we continued with the pregnancy. We still got high together, and she still worked.

During her pregnancy, I found a place to live with another family. My behavior continued, but I convinced Dee to come live with me while she was pregnant. She was not getting the prenatal care she needed, as you can imagine. I could tell the baby's weight was low. She looked nothing like Helen or my other child's mother when they were pregnant. I asked her to stop drinking and smoking crack, yet honestly, I was not in a position to tell her to stop. I could not stop myself.

One day, as usual, we were getting high together. Dee started feeling ill. She could not shake what was happening, and we rushed her to the hospital. I did not know if it was the drugs or something to do with the baby. When we arrived at the hospital in Harrison, the doctors noticed that something was extremely off. Her life was in danger. They transferred her to Tacoma General in a matter of hours. I did not go with her, but I promised to be there the next day. During the night, the baby was born. When I arrived the next day, I was told I had a son.

I did not know if this baby was mine, and I requested a paternity test. Regardless, we still went through all the motions as if I were his father until the test could come back. Before I saw my son, a nurse pulled me aside to share what to expect when I met the baby. She went on to explain that he was born weighing one and a half pounds and was only given a slim chance to live. I had never seen a crack baby before, so when I walked into the room, I was overwhelmed by all the tubes that poured out of every opening of his body. I felt sick. My stupid, selfish drug addiction had done this to him. It felt like every eye in the room was on me, accusing and judging. Their stares and attitudes were justifiable. My son lay in an incubator, jaundiced and weak. He was newly in the world and courageously fighting for his life, and I was not even fighting for my life, the life I could have had. I cried, but my tears were not heavy enough.

The nurses let me hold him. I was extra careful, because he was so tiny he could fit inside a child's shoe. Like my other children, I rocked him, tried to soothe him. I watched as he struggled to take each breath. His whole body trembled. In that moment, I should have changed my life. I chose insanity instead, doing the same thing over and over again, expecting a different result. For five weeks, Isaiah Wayne Houston lay in the intensive care unit, and Dee lay in the maternity ward beyond the typical timeframe due to the emergency birth as well as needing additional emergency services because she attempted to get out of bed, fell, and tore open her surgical incision. The hospital couldn't understand her behavior and requested a drug screening. Of course, she came back positive, and they pegged me as her hospital supplier. I know she didn't tell the staff or police anything different. Someone else had brought her dope. She had never protected me in the past; I should not have expected anything different. When that test came back positive, I knew the baby was not coming home with either of us.

**We Lost Isaiah**
After his stay in the hospital, the state placed Isaiah in foster care. It was determined that he was born four months prematurely, and the drug use is what caused him to fight for his life. I was thankful he was alive, even if he could not be with me. He deserved better.

Our little fighter was a fantastic baby. Even though we could not take him home, they allowed us supervised visits at his foster care home. During my brief time with Isaiah, he demonstrated his strength. He smiled, tried to grab and grip things like my nose and lips, and somewhere inside of me, I wanted to believe he knew or felt something was different between him and me. He was a happy baby and well cared for by his foster family. He deserved all that love and care. I wanted my family to help, almost begging for their help. I thought maybe someone could take him, but they didn't want anything to do with him, or rather, they didn't want anything to do with Dee or me. In the end, the courts allowed a military family to adopt him, and he was gone. There were promises of photos to watch him grow, but that never materialized. I hoped and prayed that he would be healthy and happy, as I have never seen him since that last day. I pray that one day he will look for me and his siblings. I hope I am still here if that time ever comes.

Because of my addiction, I lost everything that mattered in life: my marriage, my family, and my children. This was not what others were doing to me; it was what I was doing to myself. If only I could shake this demon, I would be better, yet in the meantime, my life continued as it always had when I experienced loss. I said one day I would find both of my sons. I would look them in the eye to tell them I am sorry. I would look them in the eye to see what type of men they had become, and they would look at me and see what I had become, someone they could be proud of. In those fleeting moments of clarity, I was pushing toward the sunlight.

# Chapter 9
# Losing Mom

After we lost our son, Dee and I remained together and continued our toxic cycle. We were the scratch on the broken record, never able to fully enjoy the music because of the hiccups in our lives. Everyone else could see how toxic we were with each other; nonetheless, no one could tell me how to run my life, including my mother. I had hit a very low point.

**The Last Supper**
Dee and I found an apartment near one of the parks I used to love to visit during my binges. Infested with drug users, dealers, and prostitutes, the apartment building was perfect for us, no snitches and always a continuous supply. We were not interested in a changed lifestyle. Instead, we pushed ourselves more toward what continued to hurt us.

One day, not long after we moved into the apartment, my mother reached out to me and asked me to come to dinner. She requested that I come alone. I was angry with her request, saying that if Dee couldn't come to dinner, then I wouldn't come. I did not go, and that was the last conversation I had with my mother. My mother's health had declined during my years of addiction, and her heart was failing. I wish I had gone because about a week after her invitation, she was gone.

As usual, we had binged the night away, and I awoke to someone rapping hard on my door. I thought maybe it was a neighbor, someone who had come to tell me that they had some extra supplies. Instead, the person said my mother was in the hospital. I knew I needed to see her. In my condition, I moved as fast as I could. I managed to pull myself together, thinking I looked pretty good, got in the car, and headed to the hospital. On the way to the hospital, I felt it was bad, like this may be close to the end for my mom.

When we pulled up to the hospital, I could see several of my family members standing outside. I had barely gotten out of the car when my niece approached me and said the words I was not expecting to hear. "She's gone." It felt like that final buzzer after my last high school basketball game. Even with all my might, it just wasn't enough to pull off the win. I was sucker punched. I became numb, and the voices of people trying to talk to me sounded as if they were one hundred miles away. I didn't make it on time. It never occurred to me that I would not make it on time. I would never hear her voice again, never hear her call me her baby boy, or be in her prayers again. Her life was over, and I was an orphan. No mother. No father. Everyone had left me. Who would I be without my mother? She always reminded me that I was something special. Who would remind me now?

After a while, my niece grabbed my arm and walked me into the hospital. My mother lay there cold; the light was gone. As I always did when I said goodbye to her, I leaned over and kissed her on the forehead. This was my final goodbye to my mama. As I turned to walk away, my family and I embraced. In the back of my mind, I felt like my deterioration and drug addiction were part of the heart trouble she had. I always weighed heavily on her mind and in her prayers. Then, I asked the doctor to find out what happened, maybe not to feel as guilty as one of the contributing factors to her heart trouble. The doctor assured me that she went quickly and did not suffer. He told me that she had lived a long life and had given so much from her heart to others that it finally gave out. He helped me accept my mother's death, and I thanked him. That was just like my mom. She gave every ounce of herself to whatever she was doing, including me. I'm glad she did not suffer. I knew her time would come someday, soon after my siblings moved her from the city of Renton. I had predicted she would not make it a year without the community she had built and the home she loved. I watched as she cried when they threw away several things she considered treasures. Now, the prophecy was true.

I could do nothing more at the hospital. We had to face the reality of organizing her funeral. I needed to clear my head for the next couple of days. For the first time in a long time, I made a valid effort to keep my head clear. My mama needed me. As I walked outside to return to the car and back to my apartment, I took in the beauty of the day. It was the day after Easter Sunday. It would be just like my mom, being the Christian she was, to leave the world after she had one last resurrection celebration with Jesus. Now, she would never have to see the terribleness I or this world displayed ever again. She would be in God's arms.

## The Funeral

As we prepared my mother's funeral, I was frustrated with the information I received from my siblings. According to them, she died penniless. I questioned it because I knew she had previously secured multiple accounts. Before I fell so far into the hole, she had me as a signatory on the accounts in case anything happened to her. However, when I couldn't get myself together, my name was removed, and I'm sure it was replaced by one of the other siblings' names. Whose, I am not sure, but in my opinion, it would not be far-fetched that right after her death, one of them cleared her bank accounts out. I had told her early on, live, spend all your money, and have the life you deserve. I could only hope she had listened.

Up to the time of the funeral and during the funeral, I managed to remain pretty clear-headed. Unbeknownst to me, this was a step toward my recovery. I was not completely done with drugs, but it certainly showed that I could fight harder than I had before. I remember my mom thinking it would be my daughter's birth that would push me out of the addiction; instead, it was her death that impacted me. Maybe she needed to leave, so I could not lean on her like I had done so much in the past. I was not ready to let that crutch go entirely at the time, but it was coming. My mother had placed me in God's hands.

The church where we held the funeral was a Baptist church in

Seattle, where my mother's sister was the Mother of the Church. The songs of the choir and the sound of the Hammond organ took my mother right on home to Jesus. It was just the right service for my mother. People who loved her dearly filled the pews. To hear so many stories about who she was and how she helped people provided me with a sense of pride. That was my mother they were talking about. My ex-wife, Helen, and my daughters drove from California to pay their respects. Linda was there, although she had a sick child, and so was Marlene, whom I had met after the house fire when I was a child. Also, the church was full of White people whose lives she had touched. Everyone's presence was a testament to my mother's outstretched love, and it felt good to be surrounded by so many people who loved her. After the funeral, Marlene walked up to me and said, "I'm your mother now." I called her Mom II.

As hard as it was to say goodbye to my mother, knowing she was broken-hearted over leaving the community she had built, I did think her being laid to rest in Renton as a final resting place was fitting. Though my father had broken her heart when he left, they were only a few rows from one another. She still loved him. I could visit them both when I went to the cemetery.

The funeral was over, the repast was done, and everyone was going back to their respective places. I was headed back to my apartment to be with Dee, but something felt different this time. I thought back to how my mother felt about Dee. She did not blame her for my drug problem, but certainly, when we were together, my drug and legal issues would increase.

I felt a bit lost after my mom died and stumbled around with no particular goals or plans. This put some separation between Dee and me, yet not enough. She was back to her usual antics; this time, running away with some guy. I had learned to survive without her during these periods of craziness. You would think the constant pain she caused me would be enough to get rid of her and the drug problem. The crack was still mastering us both, though a little less for me each time. Honestly, I should have suffered more severe consequences long before I did. Once, some friends and I were in a hotel room full of drugs. There was a knock at the door, and being high, someone opened the door without inquiring who was on the other side. When the door swung open, cops with their weapons drawn were on the other side. I just knew we were screwed over. Drugs lay everywhere, and no one had had an opportunity to flush or swallow what they had. When the cop looked at the warrant, they had entered the wrong room. They never filed the charges against us. In that moment, it was God's grace; yet, the time was coming.

# Chapter 10
# Round Seven: You Lose

At some point, who I wanted to hang around started to shift. It wasn't one particular incident, but perhaps the small realization that I kept finding myself in the same circumstances. As I distanced myself from other drug users, I enjoyed hanging out with the alcoholics. It was a different world with them. In the morning, they would eat breakfast at the men's shelter and then leave to panhandle at the bus stop. Everyone contributed to the pot so that they could buy beers. In the drug world, it was every man and woman for themselves. This setup seemed more like family, quite a bit safer. They cared about me, and I cared about them.

The group consisted of people like Tony, who was super friendly. His family eventually intervened, taking him back to California to help him sober up. Then, there was Rob, a brilliant man. His family intervened too; he went back home to Illinois with his mother and father. A.P. was extremely funny. He made even the most conservative person smile and empty their pocket change. Together, we hustled to get the change and bring it in for the night's bounty. Now and then, I would get drugs for myself or someone else if they came to our alley looking. Although they were alcoholics, my new friends disapproved. Like me, they knew that the drug world was much more violent. It took me a moment to realize that they would rather I do that "stuff" somewhere else. They had a level of honor and respect they desired to maintain. I understood and worked to honor their wishes.

Our crew of alcoholics grew, and we had some good times, sleeping on tossed furniture, using old grills, and pitching tents together. We had created our world, a world that very much mimicked the spirit of freedom I experienced as a boy in the woods. One day, a woman and her two sons joined our crew. Due to her mental illness and her inability to say no to men who meant her no good, she had lost their home. They survived off the monthly check the boys' father provided. Though I had great company among my alcoholic friends, the drugs were calling to me again, and I worked to get close to them. For two months, I slept in her station wagon with her, her two boys, and their dog, Ben. We ate together and drank together as if we were having a daily cookout, as if we were a family. I had become more cunning after I met Dee.

**The Man Is Dead**
Eventually, we found ourselves moving from the alleyways to setting up a homeless campsite in a park. What we appreciated about this park was that it was far enough away from prying eyes, allowing us to enjoy life freely, and that it was near a bathroom. One morning, about two o'clock, I woke up with an

urgent need to go to the bathroom. Though I was struggling with my sight, I managed to stumble toward the bathroom for release. When I arrived at the bathroom, I noticed a man lying on the dirty floor. I was irritated because he was blocking the stall door. I yelled at him to move. I knew him. I had seen him partying at a neighboring campsite. When he didn't move, I nudged him with my foot. Ultimately, I could wait no longer and squeezed past him to relieve myself. I thought he was drunk.

I thought about taking his wallet while he lay sprawled on the floor, but something inside told me not to. It wasn't very ethical, and I felt I must have a bit of honesty left in me. I finished my business and yelled at him a few more times. He didn't move, and I was concerned that he was experiencing alcohol poisoning. So, I walked to the phone booth and dialed emergency services. After I dialed emergency services, I hung up the phone and ran to my tent. Within minutes, the police and aid services arrived.

It didn't take the medics long to pronounce the guy dead. Upon hearing the word dead, spotlights hit our camp. The police walked through asking questions.

"Who was in the bathroom?"

"Who called 911?"

One of my drinking buddies, in a drunken stupor, said, "John was in there." At first, I pretended to be asleep in my tent, but they stood firm with their spotlights on the tent. My lady friend and her two boys were sleeping inside. I didn't want the police to hurt them, trying to get to me. I crawled out, and the officer asked if I had been in the bathroom and if the man was on the floor when I went. I replied, "Yes. Is he still there?" The policeman's mannerisms shifted, and his tone changed.

"No, he's dead."

I panicked, thinking they were going to think I killed him. Then, he continued, "It looks like a drug overdose." Relief flooded my entire being. How gracious God was to me. Thankfully, I did not take the wallet. With that, the officers turned and walked away. Nothing more was said about the incident. We were all partying, and he overdosed that night. That could have been me, but my mind was far from whether the incident was an example of what could happen to me. Instead, I was thinking where I could go next.

We stayed in the park a little longer until we could afford a local Bremerton hotel known for drugs and prostitution. Regardless of its reputation, it was better than sleeping in the park. We had a bed and a hot shower. I know the kids were grateful, too. While we were there, I did what I had to do to help us survive. I hustled drugs, but like many times before, I also smoked what I had. I was not proud of what I was doing because the children were present. I would never have thought of doing this in front of my children. Afterthought made me very sorrowful that I had exposed them to my habit. Later, I sincerely apologized to the children and their mother because my behavior was unacceptable. My remorse was an indication that I was moving closer to the sunlight.

**Back Again**

Eventually, my lady friend, her sons, and I moved to a rundown trailer park. Though it wasn't much, it felt like Beverly Hills compared to some of the places I had slept. Life was improving, but the drug activity was the same. And lo and behold, I was in touch with Dee again. Dee managed to finagle her way into low-income project housing. As a known criminal, I'm unsure how she managed to do it. She was one of the faces of the crack world, being involved in raids in Bremerton and Port Orchard. Regardless, I started visiting her and getting high at her house, nonchalantly forgiving her for having double-crossed me numerous times before. Her house was never empty, and it always seemed like a party was happening. With the constant barrage of guests in and out, I felt her home was perfect for a police bust. Instinctively, I knew something felt off, yet I continued to show up and do what I knew I should not have been doing.

One day, Dee said a neighbor's husband wanted some crack. Often, I had heard Dee say the wife occasionally got high, but I had never seen her smoke. It seemed strange. However, my mindset was in such disarray that I was willing to do anything to get what I needed and carried on carelessly. I went to meet the guy, and he looked very familiar to me. I asked him if we had met before. He said no, but my instinct was that he was not being truthful.

I saw a gold cross hanging from his ear, and I realized I remembered him from downtown Bremerton, where I recalled him acting suspiciously while supposedly trying to buy crack. He drove through the alley one night, asking about crack, and then said that he would be right back. He never returned. There was another time when Dee and I lived on Warren Avenue, and someone came to our house and said there was a guy named K.A.* who wanted some crack. They asked me if I could get him the crack, and that there was money and dope in it for me. I walked up to him, and there was the same guy. That was the second time I saw him, and each time, he surrounded himself with drama. He always wanted to be out in the open, and he always talked in a loud voice. I know now why he did those things. I also know that Dee was always getting in cars with different men, and something tells me that he was one of them. I put nothing past her.

He denied being the same guy, but I distinctly remembered the gold cross hanging from his ear. He told me he had a friend who would spend three hundred dollars every day if the dope was good. Stupidly, that was all that I needed to hear, and I put aside any warning bells I might have had about him. My greed and my addiction would finally get me to the place I needed to be.

**My Last Act**
Every day, I would wait for K.A.'s call at 7:30. For some reason, Dee did not want to be a part of these transactions, which is why I later believed she was involved. I went with K.A. several times, and each time, I would have him park around the corner from where I was going. When I looked back, he had eased his car closer. He always made sure he could see who I was meeting, and he'd also ask me to take some of the dope out for his use. Now, I know the crack I was getting for him was bought with police money. The crack he had me take out for

him was from that money, so he was stealing from the police. Six times, we had these types of transactions, and no problems had occurred. It was all a setup. I had always heard that if they were setting you up, they would bust you on the third delivery. The day I was busted was my seventh run. K.A. called one day when I happened to be at Dee's house. The call was earlier than normal, but he wanted to connect at our usual time. However, he wanted to meet at a particular place, a gas station. I agreed and prepared to put together the norm for his friend. I had no problem with the arrangement, completely ignoring the unusualness of the situation.

At the agreed time, I went to the gas station and used the pay phone to make the call. While I was in the phone booth, I noticed several unmarked police cars driving by slowly and looking in my direction. At that moment, I should have walked away, yet my mind remained numb to the warnings. Some of the faces in the cars looked familiar from a previous close call a while back. After several more cars passed by, I finally saw K.A. He looked at me, nodded his head, and sped off. In that moment, I knew I was done. Four cars surrounded me. The detectives jumped out with weapons drawn. "Get on the ground! Get on the ground!" I complied. My life was not worth my addiction. For thirty-six years, I had dodged what I needed most. I lay on the ground, a dog on top of me, ready to attack at the given command. Welcome to the sunlight.

*For the purposes of this book, the name of the informant was not required; thus, the informant's real name nor initials were used.*

> "I knew I was done.
>
> …
>
> My life was not worth my addiction. For thirty-six years, I had dodged what I needed most."

# SECTION III
# FIGHTING FOR
# THE SUNLIGHT

# Chapter 11
# The Choice

You have no dignity when you're lying face down on the ground for all the world to see, but I deserved to be right where I was. My habit may have started because of dealing with the trauma from my childhood, but what I had become was someone my childhood self would have never recognized. This was the ultimate feeling of vulnerability and powerlessness, and I needed it. I needed something or someone to break the power the drugs had over me.

When they picked me up off the ground and placed me in the back of the police car, I knew my life as an addict and drug dealer was over. At the police station, they offered me a deal to serve as an informant, like K.A. They said that if I worked for them, they would reduce my charges. K.A. was considered a highly valuable asset, helping the police to make around forty busts. They called his testimony liquid gold in the courtroom. I told them I would think about it if it would help waive my charges. However, K.A., a glorified errand boy, was still doing drugs himself. I needed a drastic change. Plus, I would never get away from that world. Everyone knew what it meant if you were caught snitching.

**The Ultimatum**
I later learned that Dee had been arrested, too, and I knew her arraignment was coming up soon. As I entered the courtroom, she was leaving the courtroom, and she advised me to ask for Drug Court for a reduced sentence. That was one of the only good things she could have ever done for me, besides giving birth to my child. So, I chose to request Drug Court.

When Judge Jay Roof, who was the presiding judge over Drug Court, called my name, I didn't know what to expect. He looked at my file, then looked at me and asked, "Man, what are you doing here? You're like fifty years old." I wanted to spew out something smooth, something that made sense, but when I opened my mouth to speak, I was only left with a hanging mouth. I was speechless. What was I doing there? For thirty-six years, drugs had controlled my life.

When I finally spoke, the only thing I could say was, "I don't know." For the first time in my life, I felt guilt, shame, embarrassment, and loss. Based on the charges, he explained that I was facing many years in prison. When I inquired about the possibility of Drug Court, he responded that it was a good idea, considering the potential length of the sentence. This was it for me. Prison or Drug Court, both would be a long road, but only one was prepared to give me the help I needed. What the judge didn't understand that day was that I had to make it work.

Of course, news of my arrest had spread. My family was done with me and my antics. My oldest daughter, Marisa, was pregnant with my first grandchild. I couldn't believe it. I was going to be a grandfather, and it felt like all the wind was knocked out of me when she said I could not be involved in my grandchild's life with the way I had been living. Not being able to be involved with my grandchildren and my lineage gutted me. No, I was nowhere near the excellent grandparent my mother was, but not to see my grandchild or being involved in this child's life was not an option for me. I had already lost my relationship with my two oldest children and lost both of my sons to other families. Now, I would lose my next generation, and the responsibility sat squarely on my shoulders. This was enough of an incentive for me to get clean.

When I returned to Bremerton to say my farewells, I was nervous about sharing that I had chosen to go through Drug Court. I mustered the courage, and when I shared, some laughed. Nevertheless, I had made up my mind, and I would not be deterred. They didn't understand. God had given me a glimpse of the sunlight. With my grandchild coming, I somehow felt like I was receiving a second chance at life. Everyone else knew me as this, the junkie. However, that sweet baby would only know me as the loving grandfather that I wanted to be. That baby would see me as the new man I could be. I said my farewells to everyone and returned to Kitsap County court to start the process.

## Drug Court

They took Drug Court very seriously. Truly, it was not a 'get out of jail free' card. They had an intense eighteen-month regimen and an expected outcome. I knew of one other person who had chosen Drug Court before, one of my regular suppliers. The guy was going through the program while making drops through open windows. Eventually, he was booted from the program and served time. That was not my intention. I was going to do this and do it right. Yet, before I made the final decision and signed the agreement, they allowed me to observe the program. What I saw in the program was very encouraging, and everyone there, including Dee and many others I knew, seemed to be doing well. I had a good feeling about my decision.

On my first day of drug court, I was put to the test. It was as if God were testing my willingness to succeed. Before court, I had an appointment with my ophthalmologist, who dilated my eyes. Now, being legally blind, I was particularly sensitive to sunlight and required black wraparound glasses. As soon as I walked in, I caught the eye of a guy with a ponytail. He knew exactly who I was and immediately stated that I could not wear those glasses in the courtroom. The addict in me wanted to ask, "Who the heck are you?" He looked exactly like the guys I had to fight every day growing up. Instead, I leaned over and told him about my condition. He expressed that he was unaware of my eye condition. Right then, I learned something new that helped me achieve the position I wanted. Listen and do not overreact, as the issue can be easily solved. If I had ranted or raved, I would have failed the test and never seen the completion of Drug Court.

## The Beginning of an End

As I stood in front of Judge Roof, he asked me why I wanted to join the Drug Court program. He knew of me because I had been before him in previous circumstances, which was not favorable toward me, but here in Drug Court, I had seen his compassion toward others, even though we did not like each other. In response, I mumbled something about my desire to avoid prison and change my life. I was sure it was a generic answer he had heard thousands of times. Nevertheless, he started the process by reciting the rules and requirements.

He didn't have to tell me that it wouldn't be an easy task. Others had said Drug Court sets you up for failure and encouraged me to do the time. I was not keen on taking those people's advice because I know misery loves company. They didn't want me to change. After Judge Roof recited the rules and requirements, and he was certain I had a clear understanding of the agreement, it was time to move forward. He then introduced me to Steve, the guy with the ponytail from my earlier interaction. Steve would be my counselor and ultimately become monumental in my recovery.

## Breakthrough

As part of Drug Court, you are required to attend meetings. Because I had tried AA or Alcoholics Anonymous before and failed, I decided to try NA or Narcotics Anonymous. When I arrived at my first and only meeting, I was one of the oldest guys in the room. I'm sure they strategically chose the location because it was near one of the places where I bought, sold, and used drugs. As some of the younger attendees shared their glorified stories of drugs and chaos, my cravings savagely surfaced. I knew right then that this was not the place for me. While I wasn't sure if I could become completely sober and live a clean life, and others had already told me that I wouldn't make it six months in Drug Court, I needed to prove them wrong. I needed to prove to myself that I was worth the help I was receiving. I had one more option: return to AA.

When I walked into the AA noon meeting, the room was packed, young, old, those with babies on their hips, and even some people I had known from the streets. Suddenly, I felt embarrassed, not because of the diversity of the room, but because on the street, people just called me John Wayne, my first and middle name, reflecting the strong, rugged exterior—the person no one wanted to mess with. However, here I felt weak and defeated. Despite this, people were encouraging and shared suggestions on how I could beat addiction and experience sobriety. It felt like they believed in me more than I believed in myself.

According to the Drug Court requirements, I had to attend three meetings. My attitude stunk because I refused to give Drug Court more than the three they required. Living in the trailer park now, I had to ride the bus to meetings. Having to ride the bus continuously was going to be a problem for me, but God knocked my excuse out—a man who also attended the meetings offered to give me a ride to the meetings. At first, I thought he was weird. *Why was he trying to help me?* I didn't want his help, but I eventually accepted it. Every day, he came to pick me up for those AA meetings, and I exceeded the Drug Court requirements. Then, he invited me to his home. While there, he would read the Big Book of AA. He did this a few times, and the sunlight broke through. I finally got it. This sobriety walk was a constant job, a consistent walk that required daily recognition. That was the missing element for me, and I went from a very dark and dingy place, full of vicious violence and deadly circumstances, to taking my first step into the sunlight. The more I read with him, the clearer the picture became.

> "I reflected on how much more beautiful California was than the last time I was there. Its natural scenery, vibrant culture, and artistic vibes blended seamlessly in the background as we reconnected, painting the picture of what I wanted for our family: a natural, vibrant, and easy rhythm in which we could all heal."

# Chapter 12
# The Steps

Now that I knew what I had to do to walk fully in the sunlight, I didn't think I would be ready for the twelve-step program. I was getting my first honest look at what the twelve steps were directing me to do. I had to admit my life was unmanageable and that I was powerless. I had to reconnect with my God, and I had to make amends with those I harmed. My friend didn't pressure me; instead, he assured me that he would be there when I was ready. Sports were the last thing I had consistently stuck to, and that was more than thirty years ago at this point; nevertheless, I wanted to try. It wasn't easy — taking one step, then two.

As I attended more AA meetings, I started to enjoy them. I looked forward to hearing from the guest speakers who had achieved at least two years of sobriety. I was surprised when one of the guest speakers turned out to be a neighbor from my childhood. He had worked at Boeing, a place that had divided my family from the rest of my classmates' families. His presence was a reminder that everyone faces pressure, and money does not matter when you don't know how to cope. When I met his daughter later and learned we had had some of the same teachers and knew some of the same people, I felt more comfortable attending meetings. They were not so different from me after all, and this helped me move closer to the twelve-step meeting hall.

**New Living**
During the transition to the next step of the program, I improved my living situation. I wanted to be around more people who were trying to make it. I had been in touch with one of my junior high school girlfriends, Linda, and told her of the changes I wanted to make in my life. She was elated, and with her help, I started looking for the right place to live. It was time for me to be responsible for my bills and stop living off of women.

A married couple, who worked together to get sober, told me about a landlord who had given them a chance. With my background, I was nervous even to try, yet I chose to be honest, hoping for grace. I called the landlord and set up a meeting. When I met with him, I told him the whole truth. I told him about my rental history. I told him I was in Drug Court, required to take random drug tests, and have surprise visits from my compliance officer. I also told him I was facing prison time, and failure was not an option. He agreed to give me a chance, and I took it. The landlord understandably required me to pay a large deposit and warned that if I decided to go south, I would need to leave his apartment. I understood. I would not destroy this opportunity.

## A Stream of Light

On move-in day, I only had a couple of blankets and a few clothes. Although technically impoverished, I happily slept on that floor. This was my place. That night, I just sat and listened. I remembered how I had been in this building before, in this very apartment, using drugs. I had used drugs in almost every apartment in this building at some time. Although I knew there was still illicit behavior happening, I yearned for the warmth of the sunlight on my face. Judge Roof had talked to me as if my life were worth something.

The next day, my friend, Linda, took me to a second-hand furniture store to purchase a sofa, loveseat, dining set, and TV. We also bought some additional household items at the thrift store. I was making a home for myself, and I felt good about it. If I were willing to work for it, the rewards would reveal themselves. It was a lesson I had learned as a child. The following week, Linda found a stereo system at a swap meet, and I felt like I was in heaven. I have always loved music. Now, I could sit for hours and listen to my favorites: Stevie Wonder, Tower of Power, Marvin Gaye, Eric Clapton, and many more. I was connecting with the things that I loved, the things that helped me embrace my uniqueness.

One day, Linda found a computer someone had donated. She helped me learn how to use it and navigate the internet even with my poor vision. Next came the makeover. We shopped for new clothes, not the usual old jeans and beat-up sneakers. I had my first professional haircut in years and committed to seeing the barber twice a month. We found Dr. Volz, who agreed to help fix my teeth and restore my smile for free; years of drug abuse had destroyed my teeth. When everything was done, I looked at myself in the mirror and took pride in who I saw. Now, the sunlight was streaming in through the window.

## Determined to See Olivia

As each day passed, I thought less and less about getting high. My counselor challenged me, told me my odds were slim, and, being a former athlete, I was always up for a challenge. I couldn't remember if he knew I was a former athlete; nonetheless, if he did and used this technique purposefully, it worked. I planned to beat that slim chance and the six-month bet people had made on me. I attended more AA meetings, up to four a day, if I could. I started to recognize who was there to socialize truly and those who were there to hook up. This discernment helped me steer clear of the wrong people. One of the people who was supposed to be there was Dee. Not surprisingly, I never saw her there. Although my mom couldn't see me, I knew her prayers were working, and my two aunts said so. She had prayed for a long time that this addiction would lift from my life. I truly felt that God was with me, and I was determined to rebuild my life so that I could see my children and grandchildren.

As I grew closer to people in the twelve-step program, I was able to see some fantastic results. One man, whom I affectionately nicknamed the whale walker because he was always on the move, walking the floor during the entirety of our meetings, shared how he could only walk six inches at a time when he was under the influence and searching for whales off the bridges. Being sober, he could walk five miles a day. I met another woman who suggested people who would make good sponsors for me. I was not opposed to the idea, but when she introduced me to the only two Black men in the meeting, I did not appreciate that. Not every Black man thinks the same. I declined, and the man I called the whale walker stepped in to be my friend and help guide me.

Things were going well. I had attended all required meetings and more. I was learning, gaining confidence. Yet, there was still one thing I wanted. I wanted to meet my granddaughter, Olivia. Hopeful, I told my counselor that I wanted to visit my granddaughter in California; except when I saw Judge Roof on that Friday for our weekly check-ins, he shockingly told me no and to check with him in two weeks. I was angry, but I understood. At least he didn't say no, you cannot go at all. It was another challenge. I stepped up my game even more.

When I had the opportunity, I shared that I had finally figured out what I wanted to do with my life. I told Judge Roof that I wanted to help kids avoid the same mistakes I made. I was proud of myself for knowing which direction I wanted to go in. Despite that, I was left dumbfounded when he asked me how I was going to do it. Speechless, I had not ironed out the details. He suggested I make some phone calls, saying that if I wanted to do it, I should go for it. This was a huge turning point for me. I started making the phone calls. When I returned to ask if I could see my granddaughter in California, he granted my request. I had three days. I had to call before I left and call when I returned. Also, I needed to bring a picture of my grandbaby back. I replied, "No problem." I wasn't being cocky or complacent; I knew I would do right.

**California**

It had been five years since I physically laid eyes on my daughters. I was a bundle of nerves. I shared my fears with my twelve-step group, and one of the old-timers in the program pulled me aside and advised me to go there and watch. If I acted like I was in control, they would resent me. I understood. Still nervous, I had to muster every ounce of courage to go. Linda drove me to the airport, got me to my gate, and I was off into the air. It was time for the healing to begin. No more fake apologies, it was time to meet the new John Wayne Houston.

When I stepped off the plane, my fears quickly disappeared. The first person I saw was my youngest daughter, Renee. My ex-wife, Helen, stood by her side. Already overwhelmed with emotion, I stepped toward them, and Renee met me with an embrace. Tears flowed. It had been a long time since I held my baby girl. It was so good to see her, although I wasn't out of the woods yet. Helen stood back and watched, careful not to participate. I respected her decision. She had loved me unconditionally, and I had bled all over her with my open wounds.

As we drove toward Helen's home and talked, I reflected on how much more beautiful California was than the last time I was there. Its natural scenery, vibrant culture, and artistic vibes blended seamlessly in the background as we reconnected, painting the picture of what I wanted for our family: a natural, vibrant, and easy rhythm in which we could all heal. Given my tense relationship with my oldest daughter, Marisa, I was unsure how she would react to me. Therefore, when we arrived at Helen's home and she was standing there with baby Olivia in her arms, I knew we could move forward.

When I saw my inspiration, I could barely contain myself. Baby Olivia was beautiful, with her chubby cheeks, curly hair, soft babbling, and coos. I got out of the car, and Marisa placed her in my arms. I burst into tears. This would have been the baby that I wouldn't have been able to hold if I had not stayed on track with my program. She was perfect. Holding her felt like I was in the delivery room again, lifting my children to the sky for the first time. I must have held her for at least an hour, cherishing every moment. It was a miracle having the ability to stand in my ex-wife's and her now husband's home with my family. I knew I would never go back to my old life again.

While I was there, we had a good time. I took the old-timer's advice, relaxed, and observed. I spent time with my ex-wife's new husband, Dan, who turned into one of my best friends and mentors. I am forever grateful to him for stepping up and becoming a father figure in my daughters' lives. My former in-laws visited and welcomed me back to the family. My former sister-in-law and her children visited and wished me well in my recovery. I was amid a love fest. So many tears fell from everyone's eyes. Then, my former father-in-law set the atmosphere off with one of my favorite Indonesian dishes he used to cook for me. All was well.

Before I left California, the family invited me to go to church with them. Initially hesitant, I finally agreed to go after they spoke highly of it. It was a Catholic church, and I was expecting a typical Catholic Mass - dry, dull, and religiously cathartic, although some would have called Mass services serene with deep ritualistic significance. I chose to be kind and prepared myself for the services. The whole family crammed onto the same bench and patiently waited for the organist to start. However, when the choir came down the aisle singing like they could rival any Baptist church I had ever attended, I knew this was not your typical Catholic church. Pleasantly surprised, I believe that was the day God showed me what life could be like with Him. Step one, I admitted my powerlessness. Step two: I acknowledge that there is a power greater than myself that can help me.

## Chapter 13
## All In

I left California feeling full. As we stood in a circle, saying goodbye with tears rolling down our faces and our hands joined, we prayed. On the plane home, I cried all the way back to the Seattle airport. My daughters were amazing during this whole process, and I loved them even more for their ability to forgive. They have always been a special part of my scattered life. I give God and their mother credit for allowing them to form their own opinions about me. I am glad that Helen introduced them to God, and they had the opportunity to learn forgiveness. I was at peace.

Linda picked me up from the airport, and we headed to the Kitsap Recovery Center in Bremerton. I had remembered the instructions I received. I diligently carried out every step, determined not to make a mistake. I was amazed that I did not think about getting high the whole time I was in California. I was on my way. When I saw Judge Roof later that week, I proudly walked up and showed him my beautiful granddaughter, Olivia. He kept that picture, and every time I went in front of him for the next year and a half, he asked me about her.

## Full Integration

Over the next year and a half, I worked hard during my recovery process. My niece Marie became one of my biggest supporters. Between her and Linda, I got to every place I needed to go. Marie was the daughter of my oldest sister Irma. When she was born, she and Irma stayed with Mama and me, forming a special relationship. Now, she was a part of my cheering section, pretending to call to say hello when she was making sure I was still on track. I loved that.

I fully integrated the twelve-step program into my life. I was learning to enjoy sobriety. When I walked down the street, people said "hello" or "good morning" instead of clutching their purses or locking their car doors. They were amazed by the transformation; even people from the streets were telling me how proud they were of me. I was becoming a role model, a feeling that was quite foreign to me. Surrendering and accepting my life for what it was, I made it my mission to improve my life and help others escape the grasp of whatever had taken them away from the life they were meant to live.

## Building

I had changed nearly everything about my life. I had changed myself, my attitude toward others, and my outlook. I paid attention to the small details of success, such as making my bed every morning, cleaning my dirty dishes, maintaining my grooming practices, and managing my finances. The same disability check I had once used to get drugs now paid for rent, utilities, groceries, and my "participation fee" for Drug Court. When Linda asked me what I wanted for Christmas, I chose something practical and fitting for me. I wanted a nice coat. I worked toward reconnecting with my extended family. For the Labor Day weekend, I started an annual family picnic. These successes further expanded my goals and ambitions.

As I mentioned earlier, I had decided to work with children. My first taste of what it felt like to mentor happened when I was cleared to volunteer at the Juvenile Detention Center. It was my first step to becoming the type of professional I desired to be. Talking to the youth for the first time gave me an uneasy feeling. I wanted to be open and honest, and I did not want the youth to think I only knew what I had read in books. I usually shared some of my history to let them know that I was the real deal. After that talk, I received clearance for the Boys and Girls Club. I was becoming a bright light even to some of the doubters.

My next step was to become a speaker within my group. I was nervous about speaking at the largest group session, but I laughed and cried my way through as I shared my story. Linda, my two sisters, nieces, nephews, and old drug-using friends who were trying to get sober were all there. For the first time, I felt a sense of freedom. The chains were falling. I didn't have to try to impress anyone. I was simply being me. The world was quickly opening up to me after so many years of darkness.

I was becoming a respectable person. Police officers who once stopped me, chased me, and arrested me would now stop me on the street and comment on how good and healthy I looked. Randy, the owner of one of the convenience stores, told me he was proud of me for what I was doing. Some friends from my youth would also tell me that they knew I was a good person, and they were waiting for me to come back to my senses. I could feel and see the changes in my life, and those around me could see the same.

As I followed the counsel and suggestions of my sober family-people who had successfully engaged sobriety and were cheering me on to do the same, things were going well. I called them family because their love was so unconditional. They continuously encouraged me to find the happiness that sobriety brings. Around the same time, which was the beginning of my second year sober, I received a call from the local Kitsap County newspaper, the Kitsap Sun, and a reporter wanted to do a story about my life of addiction and the things that I was doing to change my life. The story was titled "Breaking the Cycle". The reporter's genuine interest in my life story, recovery, and Drug Court encouraged me further. Almost instantly, we became friends. As he interviewed me and took pictures, who I am today was being born. While I am thankful for the article, the many articles that followed the interview, and the surprising support from people, it was another reminder of who I could be and one day would be if I kept going. And keep going, I did.

# Chapter 14
# Success Unlocked

You can never be what you can be until you try to be what you have never been. I was encroaching upon a new era in my life. The sunlight was close. I could feel the warmth on my skin. That little boy, who played in the woods, imagining himself to be a cowboy, exploring the land like the Native Americans, and building a lean-to shack with scraps, was emerging from the darkness, light piercing every aspect of my life. Now, I was imagining myself as a respected professional helping others combat the demons I faced. It had been a long thirty-six years, but in eighteen months, everything had turned around. I had four goals to achieve to reach the sunlight. First, I needed to get my high school diploma. Second, I needed to start college. Third, I needed to graduate from Drug Court. Finally, I needed to graduate from college. All were within my reach.

**The Test**
I wanted to be a youth counselor, and Judge Roof had challenged me to learn all the steps necessary to make that

happen in my life. I researched and discovered the essential steps, yet found myself hindered. Not having my high school diploma plagued my ability to move forward in my profession. I still needed that one math credit that devastatingly ended my previous dreams. Now, being legally blind, I wondered what was possible. I needed help.

Steve, my counselor, told me about this agency called Disability Services for the Blind (DSB). DSB works to integrate people with visual disabilities into the mainstream by helping them find employment and further their education. According to Steve, DSB could assist me with my school-related needs, including books, tuition, and any accommodations I needed to succeed. I picked up the phone and called. One of the biggest lessons I learned in my Drug Court journey was the importance of asking for help. When I looked back on my long history of drug abuse, I never asked for help. When I was looking for salvation, I turned to drugs. When I was feeling emotionally overwhelmed, I turned to drugs. When I failed, I turned to drugs. Failing in my marriage, I turned to drugs. Failing as a father, I turned to drugs. Drugs had become my answer to every problem I was facing. However, the real answer was to take a proactive approach to the issue and step up to ask for the help I needed if it was beyond my capacity to handle it.

When I called DSB to learn about the services they could provide for me specifically, I was paired with a counselor named Mike. When Mike learned about my history as an addict, I could sense his uneasiness, although he maintained his professional demeanor. I did not allow his uneasiness to discourage me. Instead, I freely talked about what I wanted to do and how I wanted to do it. Soon, he became one of my biggest supporters and fans.

After meeting specific requirements, such as taking the Accuplacer test, which would determine where I needed to start in my educational journey, the agency was willing to help. Honestly, I didn't know how I would perform on the placement test. Math had never been a strong subject for me, and my mind was so scrambled from the drugs that I could barely put together sentences that made sense. Anxiety crept in, stealing my peace. I could have quit right then, but I didn't. At this point, so many people were rooting for my win that I didn't want to let them down. So, I took the test.

When the results came back, they were daunting. My score was not high enough to bypass the math requirement and earn the credit. Also, I needed a remedial English course to bring me up to the required collegiate level. What was good about the situation was that I could take the classes at Olympic College. They would allow me to obtain the credits to graduate from high school and continue my collegiate journey officially. One setback was that I could not count the courses toward my college credits; despite this, I was determined. I made arrangements to move forward. Linda and Marie were by my side for the whole process.

Once I enrolled in my classes, DSB provided me with a laptop and a recorder for my audiobooks. The most essential item included on the computer was a program called ZoomText, which enlarged my text for reading. As Mike helped me obtain all the equipment I needed, he also encouraged me, and he would remain a supporter in my life for the next three years. It was time to start school. In January 2006, I began attending Olympic College to earn my high school diploma.

**Drug Court Graduation**
Days after entering college, I was set to achieve another milestone: graduation from the Drug Court program. On January 16, 2006, I proudly stood alongside other successful candidates, ready to embark on the next phase of my life. At my Drug Court program graduation, people who loved me, people I had hurt, people who supported me, and even people who didn't think I would make it all sat in the audience smiling, some with tears discreetly slipping from their eyes. My moment was their moment too. It had taken a village to get me here, one full of tough love and visions of who I could be.

When it was my turn to give my speech as a successful candidate of the program, I started with a bit of humor to avoid bawling my eyes out. I inquired, "I wondered how a White man, wearing a black dress, i.e., his honor's robe, could teach a Black man about life." The audience laughed as Judge Roof curtsied at the mention of the black dress. For so long I had run from life because I did not think my life was worth living, but as I looked over that audience and saw my family from California, my girls; my niece Marie; Marlene aka Mom II; good friends Jon, Dr. Whitney, and his wife Mary Lou, Eammom and his wife Julie, Linda, and so many others who contributed to my journey, this was community. This was love. This is how my journey was a success.

In my speech, I talked about my mother's prayers, how she

desperately wanted me to be free from drugs. "Mama, I did it. With God's help and Him surrounding me with love, I did it." Maybe she left here peacefully knowing that God would answer her prayer one day. I thanked everyone, especially those who were there during the darkest days of early recovery. Steve, my counselor, refused to give up on me, even when I made excuses, and I continued to talk to him beyond my graduation. My message was not only about my success and gratitude for the tremendous support I received, but also an opportunity to make amends. I cannot go back and change the past; however, I can go forward and impact the future. The cycle was broken. Now, I was living a life of significance. By the time I finished, I could no longer hold back the tears of joy and freedom. I wept openly; I wept bravely.

After the ceremony, we enjoyed a lovely reception at the Bremerton Waterfront Inn. At the reception, it was nice to hear so many people say nice things about me and wish me well as I pursued my high school diploma and college degree. Many shared how the newspaper article in the Kitsap Sun inspired them. The writer, Josh, had done an excellent job portraying the struggles and displaying what hope looks like in a seemingly hopeless situation. This was where I was supposed to be, among all the smiling faces and well wishes. This was me pushing into the sunlight.

**Going for the Gold**
I looked forward to the day when I could receive my high school diploma with the gold seal. With my test score and previous academic difficulties, I readily received help to ensure I finished what I started. I had no intention of repeating the

same mistake I had made with Bellevue Community College. It was tough. The dark days came, having not been in a classroom for over thirty years, yet I kept my eyes on what I wanted to achieve. And of course, Linda was beside me, cheering me on, along with my niece Marie.

The college's Access Services department provided the student support I needed to get through my classes. They were specifically designated to help students with disabilities access the resources they need to succeed in their college studies. From the moment I walked into that office, I felt a warmth similar to a bright ray of sunshine. I know Karen, the director of Access Services, and Julie, her assistant, could sense and probably see my fear and uncertainty; nevertheless, they took extraordinary measures to ensure that I understood why they worked there. Ultimately, they became an integral part of my education and a significant part of my ongoing recovery. I don't even know if they realize how important they were to me in maintaining my sobriety. The stress was real. I started calling them "My Ladies of Access Services." They became my family there at Olympic College.

For two years, I would stop by Access Services' office before class and on my way home. We would handle our school business, and then, we talked about our children, grandchildren, and, in their case, spouses. On cold, rainy, snowy, and stormy mornings, I would stop by their office, and there would be those smiles and a look that said, "Keep going." It seemed that with each step I took, God had someone there waiting for me to guide me when I arrived. It always happened that just when those thoughts of not being able to make it in school or life would hit me, a ray of sunlight would shine on my face, and I would feel God saying, "Just have faith in me. Have I let you down so far? Have faith in what you have been given, and there is more to come."

I especially needed faith to finish my math course. My first professor was known for being challenging to work with. When class started, she reminded us that we should have earned the math credit in high school. It was as if she were offended at being assigned to teach us. Also, on the first day of class, she broke my anonymity. The old me would have responded with harshness; the new me let it slide, as I wanted to be open about who I was and my newfound freedom. I wasn't the six-year-old on the playground anymore with hurt feelings.

Sometimes, she would write using a red marker on a whiteboard, which, for someone with low vision, made it impossible to see. When reminded that she was to accommodate for my low vision, she responded that she kept forgetting, even though the school had informed her. To remedy the situation, she asked me for my picture to remind her that she needed to use a different marker. Even after I gave her a picture, she continued to write in red and act as if my accommodations were an inconvenience. For example, I asked her for enlarged copies of handouts. She was not thrilled to provide the copies. A few times, she even placed the work on pink pieces of paper, knowing I couldn't see it. Although it was frustrating, I persevered.

I tried everything to succeed in her class; finally, I had to report her for the ongoing lack of accommodations. I didn't want to cause trouble. I didn't want to assert myself, but she was impeding my ability to succeed. I filed a complaint with Access Services and her director. After the formal complaint, she improved her behavior for a while. As in my teenage years, problems continued to erupt, no matter how hard I worked or tried. Then one day, she said I was failing. I knew I could not fail the class and extend my time at Olympic College. Again, I had to file another complaint. The school resolved the issue by giving me an incomplete in the course. Later, I discovered that the professor had had cancer. She was bleeding on me with her open wounds. I was glad I didn't harshly treat her with my words or behavior. Sometimes, you don't know what is happening with people.

That summer, I retook the math class under a different professor, and my experience was enjoyable. I completed the math course with a "B" average. I was shocked. The area that I felt had held me back became a hill I stood on in triumph. It happened that a woman I had known from the streets was attending Olympic College at the same time. Her name was Rhonda. Rhonda was an excellent student academically, and she volunteered to tutor me in math. What I discovered along the way was that a little extra effort helped me achieve better grades and confidence in my academic studies. God had placed Rhonda, like so many others, there at the right time in the right place. I saw significant improvement in my writing, and another course I took alongside those core subjects—a computer course—helped me obtain my first "A." I was having success, and that success fueled me.

Upon obtaining the math credit, I received my high school diploma. Years of trauma washed away. For so long, I had kept the secret that I did not have my high school diploma. Shame kept me in that dark place, but at fifty-two years old, I had had enough. It was not too late. People may say it's too late. Your mind may tell you that it is too late. However, it was not true. Now, I could start my real college career. My eyes could see the glow from the sunlight.

> "I was pleasantly surprised to see a room full of kids from all ethnic backgrounds laughing, eating, and doing their homework together. In my youth, I would have never seen a scenario like this."

# Chapter 15
# College Life

Now that I had completed my first educational hurdle, I was ready to tackle college life as a full-time student. I cannot tell you all the courses I took; however, the experiences I had were invaluable. During that time, many people heard or saw my story and were inspired by my journey. While my journey inspired them, I was inspired by the way they lent their hands to help me.

**Fitting In**
One of the people who heard my story was Rachel, the director of the Multicultural Center at Olympic College. Rachel attended the Kitsap Leadership Conference, where I was a guest speaker and shared a portion of my story. At the conference, she asked me to stop by and see her once I settled into school, as she wanted to see me succeed and would be available for advice. I don't know why I was nervous to visit the Multicultural Center, but ultimately it was for no reason. I think I was trying to figure out how I fit in with this younger

crowd, yet when I entered the center, everyone was welcoming.

I was pleasantly surprised to see a room full of kids from all ethnic backgrounds laughing, eating, and doing their homework together. In my youth, I would have never seen a scenario like this. This reminded me of how times had changed, how people had changed. A part of me was still stuck in the 1960s ideology of what education looked like for a person of color, and here I was standing amid change that many had preached and fought for. After Rachel introduced me to the students, I felt completely at ease. These students were younger than my children, and I know I was closer to the age of most of their grandparents. Despite this, Rachel assured me that someone would always be present to help tutor me. You know what, no one ever considered my age. I felt a sense of belonging and acceptance that I had not experienced in a long time.

Rachel remained committed to my success, and one day, she invited me to attend the annual Student of Color Conference held in Yakima. Once more, I was hesitant. Forty students from Olympic College, a total of six hundred students from across the state, would attend this conference. I was hesitant because of my age and disability. Once again, Rachel reassured me and convinced me that the experience would be unforgettable. She was right.

Riding on the tour bus with forty college students was a blast. We played a game where we switched seats throughout the trip, allowing us to learn more about each other. I learned a lot, especially about those who had chosen to attend Olympic

College versus college in their home countries. Throughout the trip, everyone treated me the same; no one mentioned my age or disability. In my pursuit of a college education, I never thought I would have the opportunity to gain experiences beyond the classroom. These experiences were enriching and helped me build a community on campus, a community I needed to help me reach wholeness in who I was as a person.

At the conference, I had the opportunity to step out of my comfort zone and attend exciting breakout sessions, some of which were closely related to my field of interest. The two sessions I enjoyed the most were those that dealt with drugs and gang violence, as well as the one about the lyrical impact of rap. These sessions provided information that would be most valuable later in my career. As I milled around from session to session, everyone treated me as if I were another college student. I had no reason for fear. During one of the sessions, I got a chance to speak to a room full of young people about how drugs and alcohol evaporated any ideas about college after high school and how they ruined a promising career. After I spoke, I got a standing ovation. I was simply amazed by how these students responded to me. You think you won't fit in. You question what you have to offer. Remarkably, you may find that you have more in common than different, and you will discover that each interaction provides something the other needs. We are all valuable. They needed to hear my story, and their applause reminded me that the real me was required.

As the conference concluded and we gathered for the closing ceremony, the conference leaders drew door prizes. Out of the six hundred students in attendance, my name was drawn as the grand prize winner. I won an iPod. That was my first step towards a college career that would be filled with many highlights. From that day on, I was known as "iPod John" by the students of The Multicultural Center. I can still hear the chants. I expected exclusivity, and everyone included me as one of them. Besides AA, I don't think I have had such a positive experience of inclusion. Their actions enabled me to relax and thoroughly enjoy my college experience. Just as Rachel said, my experience was unforgettable.

**Scholarship**
I could have taken my academic career in many different directions. Like any college student, I had to decide which direction would get me closest to where I wanted to be. There was no direct path to what I wanted. I thought about the Chemical Dependency Professional (CDP) program. Upon completion of the program, you receive a certificate. However, people pushed me to do more. They would not let me settle. Thus, I set my sights on an associate's degree in Arts and Sciences with an emphasis in Family Services and a certificate in Drug Counseling. Those who advised me wanted to expand my opportunities to garner opportunities within the school system.

Throughout the degree and certification programs, I listened attentively, asked questions, learned to study effectively, completed my homework, and passed my tests. I could not believe the success I was having, thinking about all the days I had failed. Who was this John Wayne Houston? I thought about all the years I could have had this, and I was thankful that the drugs had not destroyed all my brain cells. Then, it happened. I made the honor roll and Dean's List twice. After seeing my success, people suggested I apply for an academic scholarship. Now, I thought it almost seemed preposterous, but this was the era of trying new things that could bring me success.

I applied for the scholarship, wrote an essay which included portions about my journey to sobriety, and won! I won! My essay, volunteer work, and GPA were the key factors in securing the Herbert Goodman Scholarship, the most prestigious scholarship awarded at Olympic College at that time. I could not believe this was my life. To accept my scholarship, I attended a ceremony at the Admiral Theater in Bremerton. Among those present were the President and Vice President of Olympic College, donors of the scholarships, and community business leaders. I was sure many of them had seen me wander the streets of Bremerton when I was deep in my addiction, and I know some had seen my story in the Kitsap Sun.

As I accepted my award, I walked proudly yet humbly. My hard work had contributed to this moment, and it was God who had opened the door and sent the people to encourage me. It was as if He were winking, saying, 'I know what you've gone through. Now, I am fixing it.' In my teens, my thoughts were on a basketball scholarship, and here I was receiving an academic scholarship. I fully acknowledge that this did not have to be me. God could have chosen someone else. Instead, He continued to surprise me with other victories. On a different occasion, I was presented with a leadership award at the same venue. The pride my family and friends felt as I continued to excel motivated me further.

**Why Me, God?**

I initially enrolled in college as a way of breaking the negative cycle. I know that if a child excels in school and has positive role models, they have a better chance of avoiding the pitfalls they are likely to face later in life. My AA family was also there as a reminder that anything is possible and to make sure that I did not forget how I got to that stage. As God continued to work in my life, each day the sunlight was brighter than the day before. The song "Devotion" by Earth, Wind & Fire has always been an inspiring song to me, talking about brighter days, smiles, and blessing the children. I realized that I had become devoted to succeeding in college with the hope that in the future, I would be able to pass on my blessings to the children.

As I continued my journey, traveling this newfound path, the stars in the night sky shone more colorfully. Those dark hours right before dawn were not as dark. I think God was telling me all along that all I had to do was have faith, and even the darkest times were not as bad as they seemed. He was right. I earned several additional awards while attending Olympic College and maintained a GPA of A throughout my academic career.

While still in college, I was invited back as the alum speaker for the Drug Court graduations, and that was an exciting time. The first time I went back, one of the local newspapers was present and interviewed me, further demonstrating to the community that Drug Court is an effective program. Without

Drug Court, I would have gone to prison at a high cost to the taxpayers and would not have received treatment. Other invitations I received included two statewide conferences representing Olympic College. One was titled "The Faces Behind the Numbers," which aimed to showcase the successes of students at the junior college level to the state and the public. There were students from all over the state, and some had fascinating stories of overcoming poverty, complicated lives, and other obstacles to attend college. I thought about my life's turnaround and journey through Olympic College and wondered. "Why me?" Why was I the one who God allowed to take this path toward the sunlight? Why did Judge Roof, knowing that I was facing years in prison, enable me to go to California to visit my children? Why did he let me into Drug Court instead of sending me to prison? Why did my ex-wife and my daughters seem so eager to accept me back into their lives, and why did Linda, after all of the pain that I caused her, instantly offer her help towards my recovery?

At one of the drug court graduations later in the year, I was honored to share my story with politicians, judges, police officers, and citizens of Kitsap County who were evaluating what Drug Court could accomplish. Some of these same judges had sentenced me, and some of the police officers had arrested me. Now, here I was, a Drug Court graduate and a college student, studying to become a drug and alcohol counselor, speaking to those who were about to graduate from the program. I get goosebumps even now when I think about that speech.

## Graduation

I had earned my high school diploma, graduated from Drug Court, and I sat on the brink of my college graduation. I vividly recall the fear and doubts I felt when I started college. Despite my worries, I had done it. I had broken forth to live in the sunlight. An "A" average, several awards, and multiple recognitions, this was the new John Wayne Houston. Because I wanted change, every aspect of my life had changed, and I was determined to help others change their lives. As I stood on my college graduation day, I looked at how I had graduated in life.

In my early life experiences, people told me I wasn't enough, that I wasn't capable. However, I was capable. I was capable of being who God called me to be. I was capable of being significant in other people's lives without a basketball in my hand. I was capable of winning at life, and I am thankful that God sent people along my journey who saw that I could be more than what the world said I was. Maybe, in their world, I was not enough, but I don't have to be in their world. My world, this reality, the grades, the scholarships, and how people viewed me as a leader showed me that I was always enough. I did not need drugs or other people's approval; what I needed was already inside of me. I only wanted people to accept the light in me, to tell me that it was okay for me to shine in their presence. I never imagined that I would recover, let alone earn my high school diploma or a college degree. When I calculated the total miles I walked to earn that college degree, I figured it was over 2,000.

On graduation day, everyone who was significant in my life was present. It was Father's Day, and Judge Roof came. Of course, my daughters were there, as were my nieces and nephews, Mom II, Marlene, and friends like Dr. Richard Whitney, Jon Morriss, and Linda. I knew every soul there was proud of who I had become and was ready to see me move to the next level of my life. Sunlight brings growth where flowers bloom. Sunlight brought joy and eased my pain. I rose with the sun, and I finally got it right. My mind and soul were at rest, and my life was filled with good things. I had returned to the sunlight!

John Houston's Graduation Day
from Olympic College
Photo provided by Marisa Houston Alton

John Houston and his daughters
on Graduation Day
Photo provided by Marisa Houston Alton

John Houston and Judge Roof
on Graduation Day
Photo provided by Marisa Houston Alton

# SECTION IV
# LIVING IN
# THE SUNLIGHT

# Chapter 16
# Carving the Path

Even if you don't know how to get there, start moving toward what you want. When I was in Drug Court, I told Judge Roof that I wanted to work with children, to help them avoid the pitfalls I had fallen into. He challenged me to find out how I could fulfill this dream. I never thought it would lead to returning to the school system where it all began, or to creating my own nonprofit and starting my own business.

**Internship**
While I was still in Drug Court, I volunteered at the Boys and Girls Club and the Juvenile Detention Center, sharing my story. I loved being at the Boys and Girls Club. The students were always full of life, having fun, eating their snacks, showcasing their creativity, learning what it meant to be on a team, and receiving the help they needed with their homework. To be among them and see how they were able to be themselves was freeing. It reminded me of elements from my childhood—being on a team and using your imagination to be

creative—while also speaking to aspects I wish I had, such as the freedom to be myself outside of home.

On the other hand, the Juvenile Detention Center was a stark contrast to the freedom the children experienced at the Boys and Girls Club. At the detention center, they were still afforded an opportunity for education, but with a focus on rehabilitation, safety, and the ability to become productive adults, rather than integrating fun to show them who they could be. These students had already started to veer off the most promising path. Despite their circumstances, I still enjoyed spending time with them and answering their questions. In both scenarios, the children needed someone like me who had experienced both addiction and sobriety so they could understand that they could choose better.

While I was in college, I continued to volunteer and share my story with as many as were willing to listen. Perhaps, my most impactful statements were to those who were in drug-infested homes. I could always tell which children came from those types of homes because they clung to you. Emotional neglect is always guaranteed to happen in a drug-infested home.

My hard work as a volunteer paid off, as the detention center offered me an opportunity to serve as an intern after graduating from college. Here I was in my fifties, experiencing the same path as my graduating counterparts. Again, who would have thought this would be me? I didn't let my age hold me back. I fully embraced the opportunity and worked with as many children as possible. Unfortunately, it would not turn into the full-time position I wanted. I ran into some racist rhetoric, and no longer being the little boy who was afraid, I stood up for myself and the children. I felt it was my obligation to show the children that you can be more than what they say you are. In the end, I filed a complaint, and I left. Despite this unfortunate seeming setback, I was not discouraged from my quest to find the correct position for me and continued to look for other ways to serve the children.

**Outside My Comfort Zone**
After I left the Juvenile Detention Center, I obtained a job with the Pierce County Alliance, an agency in Tacoma. My previous stint in Tacoma involved a drug-infested nightmare. Now, I was returning as a success story to serve as a drug and alcohol counselor. It was hard leaving my home to move to Tacoma, as I was comfortable and had all the support I needed right there in Kitsap County, but I wanted to take on this challenge. With the help of friends, I moved and started my new journey.

When I arrived at Pierce County Alliance, it was a huge agency, the biggest I had seen or ever volunteered at. They were certified to work with individuals who suffered from drug dependency, needed mental health therapy, and were youth in state custody through the foster care system. Additionally, they collaborated with the court through deferment programs and probation, similar to the services I received through Drug Court. Thus, having the opportunity to serve within this agency was phenomenal.

During my time there, I gained invaluable experience that I

would later utilize in establishing my own nonprofit and business. However, I noticed an immediate flaw in their system. They shut down at a specific time daily, on weekends, and for holidays. Why was this a flaw, you may wonder. Being a former active addict, I know these were the hours when clientele would need you the most. It was in the lonely hours that a person was at the most significant risk of using drugs. However, six months later, my position ended due to budget cuts and my lack of seniority. I was devastated. I had moved and placed everything I had into pursuing this position. Though disappointing, I continued my quest. It may seem the hardest time happens when you are in the sunlight, but you have to keep on moving to reach the place where you want to be.

**The Struggle**
After I lost my job at Pierce County Alliance, I scoured the internet for other possible positions. Thankfully, my social security check covered my rent and food costs. I continued to trust God in the process, and I had no thoughts to get a fix to fix my emotional struggle. Instead, I reminded myself that I only needed patience. While I waited to encounter the right opportunity, Linda suggested that I take a trip to California to visit my children and grandchildren. Whenever I saw their smiling faces, it always lifted my day. It was exactly what I needed to experience refreshment and continue pursuing my goals. Sometimes, it won't come easily, but if you trust God and remain patient, it will come. I was living in the sunlight, and my days were still bright.

What I learned to do in the process of waiting was to occupy my time with positive activity. During this time, I began writing letters in the hope of inspiring others, formulated the basis for this book, and became increasingly involved with the local community, helping people achieve their goals. Some days, I cried, but triumphant ideas, such as creating a brochure about myself as a speaker, would lead to opportunities to speak, like at the middle school where three hundred students participated in a day-long event featuring me as the speaker. You must know that even if you are living in the sunlight, you will still have difficult moments. You must decide whether to embrace the sunlight or let the darkness in. I wanted the sunlight to remain, so I kept pushing.

I sent out several resumes. Between sending resumes, I road-tripped across the state of Washington and other places that interested me. We visited places like Coeur d'Alene, Idaho; Eastern Washington; Grand Coulee Dam; Omak Stampede; and the Colville Indian Pow Wow. I spent many days at Ocean Shores, and I remembered how I used to go there to party and be obnoxious to its citizens. Not now. People were experiencing the new John.

Finally, my resume campaign paid off. I received and accepted a job with a treatment facility in Mt. Vernon. The agency would soon open an office on Whidbey Island, and the job would include working as a juvenile Drug Court counselor as the lead counselor. I never thought I would hear those words, lead counselor. The pay was good, and I would be living on Whidbey Island, which is the gateway to the San Juan Islands.

I moved to Oak Harbor and found a great place to live, which had everything I wanted at the time. I always said it would be great to have a water view, and here was this condo with a view of Puget Sound and some of the smaller islands. Nature trails, eagles, and deer surrounded me. I could walk for miles along the beach. I was in God's country. That little boy inside me lit up with remembrance of my love for the woods, nature in general, and learning how people had lived off the land. At some point, I discovered that my passion for nature and history was closely associated with cultural anthropology and environmental studies. While I breathed in the beauty around me, I somehow knew I would not be here forever. As it turned out, though, it would become the place where I gained my most valuable experience yet.

**Transitioning Home**
What happened next was truly an act of God, proof that hard work pays off and dreams become reality. I received a phone call from Puget Sound Educational Service District (PSESD) informing me that I had an interview in West Seattle for a counselor position. When I went in for the interview, it went very well. I definitely tried to sell myself as the best fit for the job, especially after they told me that the position might become available in the Renton School District. I knew the interview had gone well when they called me back for a second interview with the team in Renton. I was close to realizing my dream, helping kids where I grew up. Twice, I visited with PSESD and the lady who would serve as my future boss. When I got the job, I could not express my elation in words. It felt incredible! What I had dreamed of, going back to where it all started, had happened. The sunlight was so strong that I was drawn back to my hometown.

I left Whidbey Island with some wonderful memories. I was grateful that they tried to convince me to stay, but I couldn't pass up this opportunity to go home. Just five years after being arrested, face down on the ground with a dog on top of me and no dignity, I was returning to Renton as a Prevention/Intervention Specialist and Student Assistance Counselor for Renton, Lindbergh, and Black River High Schools in the Renton School District. Everyone welcomed me with open arms. The level of warmth I felt was quite indescribable. It was as if everyone knew me, but for the right reason. I basked in that sunlight with my face toward the sun, soaking in all that I could.

I found a lovely apartment in downtown Renton, close to the bus and within walking distance of one of my schools. Moving back to the place where I grew up felt like a full-circle moment. I walked along the Cedar River trail, the same river that I floated down on inner tubes as a kid. I walked around the base path of the Little League field, where I wore my VFW uniform. I visited the gyms at Renton, Linbergh, and Hazen schools, where I spent an endless amount of time playing basketball. I ate at Jack's, a locally owned restaurant, where some of the booths feature pictures from my high school team. The person who carried the most power in my life was my mother. My mother, father, and many other family members are buried at Greenwood Cemetery right here in Renton. As I looked out my window and wrote, I could see the place where we buried my mother. Musician Jimi Hendrix is also buried at Greenwood Cemetery, but Rachel Houston is my superstar. I felt closer to her than ever, and I know she's happy to have me come home. My mother always wanted her children to do well and make her proud. She wanted to know that her work was not in vain. I hope that I have, in some way, finally made her proud. I can now visit her and the rest of my family regularly.

Since I have returned to Renton, I have found an AA group within walking distance of my house. I met an old friend from about forty years ago at my first meeting, and he put me in touch with my first-grade friend, Jim, and his family. At the schools, there is an appreciation for my knowledge and experience. Schools are infested with drugs, and my job as a prevention/ intervention specialist is to prevent and intervene in a student's drug use. We want to cut short the students' drug experiences. If a student has already started using, we want to intervene and provide that student with the help they need. If a student has not tried drugs, we want to prevent them from doing so. I have groups in all three of my schools to get these students educated about the dangers of drug use. I get to be involved in recovery, which benefits me, and I also have the opportunity to educate and mentor others. I was extremely excited about this job and the chance to contribute to my community.

**Becoming What I Needed**
While working with the Renton School District, I thoroughly enjoyed the work I did for the children. Like I had noticed with other agencies, though, the children needed support beyond the school walls. Thus, I started a nonprofit that provided after-school assistance to at-risk children. Through my nonprofit, we offer homework assistance, mentorship, afternoon snacks, and weekend snacks to those who face food insecurity. Additionally, I started a business where I counsel

youth who are involved in the court system. All of my experience was exactly what I needed to provide ongoing help for the youth in my area. I became for them what I needed the most when I was in high school. I left the school district to focus on my work full time.

Sometimes, I look back and am simply amazed that this is my story. I became a voice for the voiceless. Honestly, that is what I felt growing up, voiceless. If I had had the connection I have with children today, maybe I would have chosen a different path. But as we know, all things work together to produce a specific outcome. My path was forged through my struggles so that I could help someone else.

"My parents had built a life, bustling business ventures, and a reputation for providing some of the best pork in the state. People traveled from all around to buy from the Houston Family Farm. Had they been properly advised, I know my father would have never sold our land."

# Chapter 17
# One More Wrong to Right

In 1968, amid the greatest fights of the Civil Rights Movement, my family experienced a case of what I called "strong-armed robbery" committed by the Renton School District. This criminal act robbed me of my childhood home, my legacy, and broke up my family. Every day, I had to walk past the land where I had freely played, learned important life lessons, and thrived, knowing what had happened to my family. After I righted the wrongs in my life, it was time to right the wrongs on behalf of my family.

**The Signing**
My family suffered through house fires and a bomb. Each time something horrific happened on our land, the Renton School Board showed up to purchase our land. It was more than suspicious. However, because my father and mother could not afford an attorney, my parents struggled with what to do. How much longer would our family remain threatened? What could happen next? Who would lose their life because they didn't get

what they wanted? In the end, I know my parents did not want us to be hurt because of a piece of land, but that land was everything my parents had hoped for our family.

My parents had built a life, bustling business ventures, and a reputation for providing some of the best pork in the state. People traveled from all around to buy from the Houston Family Farm. Had they been properly advised, I know my father would have never sold our land. With a third-grade education and the inability to read, he signed an X for his signature, giving away the dream that my mother and he had worked so desperately for. With that signature came the devourment of our family, the loss of me having a father in my life, and everything they desired for our family legacy to become in this physical realm. Spiritually, my mom always wanted us to have Jesus.

When my father was around, we might have dabbled in trouble, but being the father he was, we knew we could only go so far. He was the strong figure every child needs, but they kept hammering at the nail until the wood split all the way through. Then, people hammered me until I split all the way through. To them, they took a piece of land, but for us, they set in motion years of destruction that we have yet to recover from fully- one signature and lifetimes of pain.

## Confronting the Renton School Board
With a clear head and a steady life, I, along with others in my family, wanted to do something about this wrong. Thus, we went to the Renton School Board. Some argued that eminent domain never occurred. Others say a simple threat is not

enough to make someone sell their land. However, everyone was aware of the level of tension that existed for Black Americans at the time. Would the land be worth losing your life over? They knew the house was full of kids when these heinous acts occurred. We went to school with their children. Yet, even today, some show no shame for what was done. They keep saying it was all done legally and even speak of a White family whose land was also obtained. Did that family suffer fires or bomb threats, question whether their family was still alive on that rainy night? Our land was the most prominent and prosperous plot, cleared by hand and developed to teem with life.

I know the pain I felt as I passed the land every day walking from school, and again, I could only imagine what my father felt, which is why I know that he could not bear to be in the city. You leave one state to start fresh, and once again, your life is threatened, even though you have truly done nothing wrong. We asked people to hear us. Friends and other loved ones have stood by us and demanded a rectification for what was done to our family. The value of that land is revealed by the millions of dollars worth of homes that sit on it today. I still pass by that land, remembering how my parents acquired it, making it a part of our family's history forever. Ironically, I cannot afford to live on the land where these homes now sit. We were rich, and our wealth was stripped from us.

## SB 5142

I understand that nothing can be done to bring my father back, restore his and my mother's dream for us, or replace the childhood experiences we lost as a result of losing the land.

However, I wanted the world to know our story and put a stop to practices that disproportionately affected African-American families. Now, living in the sunlight, I could walk this path and fight for my family.

On January 7, 2025, Senator Bob Hasegawa of Renton introduced SB 5142, which is also known as the Houston Eminent Domain Fairness Act. In this act, property owners will have an opportunity to repurchase their land when school districts utilize eminent domain to purchase but not use the land for its intended purpose. Although I wish we still had the land and could build our history there, this was one way to invest in the futures, dreams, and livelihoods of other families. On February 25, 2025, the Washington Senate passed the bill unanimously. On April 9, 2025, it passed in the Washington House of Representatives. On May 12, 2025, Governor Bob Ferguson signed it into law. For me, it validates the fight and the struggle we went through—no more easy pickings.

**Fulfilling Purpose**
It has been a two- or nearly three-year journey to recognition and recover some justice for my family, but I know it would not have been possible if I had not walked into the sunlight. When we are out of the sunlight, we have to ask ourselves what is happening. We were created with purpose. How can I fulfill my purpose, help my family, or others when I choose to allow the darkness to encase me instead of mustering the strength to fight back? My mother was right. We should have fought or rebuilt, not allowed the pain to overwhelm us until we fell deeper into the darkness. I know her faith in God taught her that. Now, I have that in me. It has been by God's grace that I

was able to stand before a school board, senators, and others to share my story. However, if I had not fought for that sunlight, none of this would have been possible.

This is only a portion of my story. Much more is there to write. I have grandchildren who are just starting in life. Personally, reparation for the land would help me contribute to my grandchildren's college education, like many other grandparents do. "They wanted the land for educational purposes." Maybe we can still divert the proceeds for educational purposes. We will continue our fight, and I know that I will be able to do it with a clear mind and vigor as I remain in my sobriety.

John Houston standing near the land
that was once his family's land
Photo by Gary Palmer

John Houston's family once cleared
the swampy lands of the area to reveal
the beauty it could produce
Photo by Gary Palmer

John Houston points to the woods where he often played
Photo by Gary Palmer

# Chapter 18
# My Challenge to the Future Ahead

Concluding this book, my heart swells with gratitude due to the many blessings in my life. In many ways, this is merely the beginning of an incredible journey. As the youngest son of a Louisiana sharecropper and a domestic worker who became pig farmers, I have become their hope for the future. Many ask why I didn't come into the sunlight sooner. My reply is God's timing, not mine. Often, we try to pull ourselves out of the miry clay before doing the work necessary to live the life intended for us. Darkness encased me, and I had to go to the deepest depths before I could see how devastating it was to live that life. This had to become my testimony so that I could help others. Now, doing what is right and what God has planned for me is the same.

I share my story to inspire the hopeless, those on the verge of giving up, and for the individuals who don't know how to connect with the right people to get the help they need. I share my story to encourage parents not to stop praying, law enforcement to keep believing in a better society, and for the world to know that everyone has at least one more fight in them, which is enough to win. Alcohol and drugs were the symptoms of the issues that resided deep within—unhealed hurt, pain, and unforgiveness.

For thirty-six years, I walked in that darkness, and I don't want that for anyone else. I hated myself, my life, what people said I was not, and how people devalued me based on my skin color. Hate can become all-consuming if you don't take control. However, this testimony is a recognition and realization of an all-powerful God, the one who is still hearing prayers from our mothers, fathers, and other ancestors, who saw us being and doing greater things, to give peace to those who wonder if change will ever come. Yes, that change can come. I wasn't born by a river like Sam Cooke sang of, but I was born a Houston, into a family full of hopes and dreams. The route may not have been smooth, and obviously, I was off course for quite a long time. However, I am here now, being who I was always intended to be —a beacon to help change lives.

From friends and family, I learned that power and greatness reside within each of us, and whether you are African-American, Caucasian, Native American, Asian, or of another ethnicity, we all have a choice about whether we will allow the greatest version of ourselves to rise. God gives us the power and strength to carry love, to reflect the beauty of the sunlight. When I can share my happiness and peace with those who still have an addiction, I feel that I am sharing what God has given me. In this, I am free. In five years of light, I undid everything thirty-six years of darkness stripped from me. I reflect on my college years, when I graduated with honors and a 3.8 GPA, despite having barely passed with mediocre grades in high school. I look at how crowds come to a standing ovation without me having a basketball in my hand. I look at the admiration in my children's and grandchildren's eyes for the man I have become, and no longer need the recognition of others to know that I am enough. I was made enough.

My story is not unique. Thousands have suffered immeasurably more than I have. Regardless, a place exists for all of us to reside in the sunlight. I smile as I think about how strong my daughters are. I love that, as a grandpa, I get no rest when I'm around my grandchildren because they want to show me everything, and they're crawling all over me. I have seen nieces, nephews, great-nieces, and great-nephews thrive, attend college, and lead prosperous lives. I have inspired so many people to fight for the life they are meant to live.

Whether you have dealt with racists or some other hateful group of people who don't believe in you, you have to choose. Will you let their darkness consume you, or will you shine brighter? Don't let them put out your light. Pull others into the light with you when you can. Don't let them define who you are and say what you cannot be. Only you and God should have that discussion. Then, let your voice be heard wherever you go. They don't get to choose for you. As I reflect on all my experiences, my mind drifts to "Stand" by Sly and the Family Stone, "Here Comes the Sun" by The Beatles, and "In My Life" also by The Beatles. I am proof that no matter what life throws your way, you can walk in the sunlight. This is the challenge I issue to you: Live in the sunlight!

John Houston in his office
Photo by Gary Palmer

# Special Acknowledgements

Many people have contributed to the journey that has shaped who I am today. How can I truly express my gratitude? You have been the pulse behind the beams of the sunlight. For this, I want to acknowledge you especially. Thank you. - John

Alex Monillas
Amber Riley
Annette Holmstrom and Bill
Archie and Tara Guzman
Autum Scott
Babe and Corinne Lucotch
Barry Taylor
Beatrice Hawkins and daughters
Beth Ann Perry
Betty Houston
Bill and Debbie Hansen
Bill Halseth
Bill Hansen
Bob and Pat Hall
Brad Hupp
Cal and Denice Medgard
Callen Wayne Hudson
Candace Cast
Carolyn Johnson
Cary Pencovic
Chad and Mary
Chuck Easton
Clifford Donley
Dan Stevens
Dan Bissonnette

Dana Conole Conrad
Danielle, Meagan, and Avery Woodward.
Danny Sandoval
Dave and Barbie Graves
Dave and Candace Feinberg
Dave and Lani Treece and Family
Dave Jones
Dave Skelton
Debbie Jordan
Debbie Lindgren
Debbie Phinney
Delores Blood
Denis Law
Dominick Garcia
Don and Denice Dundas
Don and Karen Torkelson
Don Anderson
Eamonn and Julie Anderson
Emilio Castillo
Ericka Bush
Ernestine Rombouts
Esther Donahue
Evan and Ali
Ferdinand Hoyer
Frank and Debra Reed
Fred Ham
Gabriel Garcia
Gay Lee
Geoff Monillas
Greg Towery
Gus Swanson
Hamish Anderson
Hazel Johnson
Helen Hoyer Stevens

Henry Stewart
Hugh and Carol Crozier
Irma Houston
Isaiah Mark Houston
Jan Stensland
Jeff Hupp
Jeff and Betsy Hummer and Family
Jerry Evans
Jil Lucotch
Jim and Jill Hall
Jim Houston
Joan Baltz
Joanne Lee
Joanne Pearson
Joel Wolsky
Jose Garcia
Josie Hoyer
Kai Johnson
Karen Jorve
Kathy Austin
Kathy Spellman
KD Seeley
Keith and Lindsey Fekette
Ken and Emily Weaver
Kevin Dickerson
Kirk and Patty Kohlrus
Kristi Towery
Larry and Jaymee Armstrong
Leroy Houston
Linda Medina
Lori Luft
Loring Larsen
Lou Cesaro
Louella Red
Lynda Muenzer

Marie Houston
Marisa Houston
Mark Monillas
Mark Wolsky
Marques Johnson
Marquesha Johnson
Mary Burns
Mel Lansing
Melinda Brown
Mike and Sue Moeller
Mike Bronson
Mike Burgess
Mike Crawford
Mike Kaufman
Mike Kever
Milagros Thompson
Mirelle Cohen
Mona Johnson
Nancy Hash
Nancy Souza
Nick Keithley
Nicole and Ellie
Nina Houston
Olivia Garcia
Pat Stevens
Pierre Hudson
Randy Ramos
Rayonna Tobin
Renee Houston Pearson
Rob Pearson Jr.
Robbie Rhett Pearson
Rocco Prestia
Rock Burns
Roger Smith
Rose Monillas

Sam and Barbara Ham
Sam Jaswal
Sandy Lawrence
Savannah Jo Pearson
Scott and Sheryl Gray
Scott Breithaupt
Scott Breithaupt Jr.
Shawn Richmond
Shaylynn Houston
Sheryl Friesz
Shirley Phinney
Steve and Laura Keithley
Steve and Pam Gray
Steve Browning
Steve Khort
Steven Miller
Student Services at Olympic College
Tara Burns
Tasha Johnson
Taylor Jaswal
Terrick Sims
Terry and Ione Smith
Tim Lambro
Tim Phinney
Tom and Debbie Lambro
Tom and Margot Grave
Tony and Stefani Jaswal
Vance Newton
Vicki Hewitt
Willard Richmond
Zariah Houston

www.ingramcontent.com/pod-product-compliance
Lightning Source LLC
Chambersburg PA
CBHW070550170426
43201CB00012B/1785